# Hitler's Obersalzberg

## Stage of World History

by Clemens M. Hutter

# The Author-Rague

Clemens M. Hutter, Ph.D. (philosophy, political science, sociology), is an Austrian journalist, author and former Fillbright Scholar in the U.S.A. The main emphases of his three dozen books are economical and social history. Hutter has a solid reputation due to his publications about fascist and Marxist-Leninist totalitarianism.
He was awarded numerous prizes for journalistic and literary achievement.

## Impressum

Translated by Ted Hassinger
©1997 Berchtesgadener Anzeiger Publishing House
Revised edition 2008
Unauthorized printing forbidden. All rights reserved.
Printed in Germany
Total production: A. Miller & Sohn KG, formerly Berchtesgadener Anzeiger,
Postfach 1153, 83461 Berchtesgaden

ISBN 3-925647-19-8

# Stage of World History

Adolf Hitler: „For me the Obersalzberg became something quite wonderful. I completely fell in love with this landscape. Here were the most beautiful times of my life. My great plans have emerged here."

And also the plans to unprecedented crimes.
Hitler not only stroked children, but also concocted the wars of aggression against Poland and the Soviet Union on the Obersalzberg,

Here he not only received statesmen and diplomats, but also orchestrated politically the annexation of Austria and the Sudetenland as well as the destruction of the rest of Czechoslovakia.

Hitler not only hosted charmingly elegant ladies at the Berghof, and as circumspect man of the house he even examined the placesettings before festive meals; here — in front of hundreds of industrialists - he also placed his suicide escape in prospect if the war were lost.

Hitler not only frolicked with dogs and fawns on the Obersalzberg. He also planned the „Final Solution of the Jewish Question" - the first industrially organized mass murder in history, whereby 6 million people were exterminated.

Hitler not only fell in love with the Obersalzberg, he abused it for a self-staged image as affable vacationer, as animal lover, and as a sociable host. He abused it as a tool to alleviate the image of mass murder, war crimes and high treason.

On the Obersalzberg nobody was tortured, strangled, stabbed, shot dead or gassed; here was neither Dachau nor Auschwitz; here nobody soiled their hands with blood.

Thus Obersalzberg became daintified as Hitler's peaceful holiday domicile. This was the perfect disguise for the most perfidious, bureaucratic perpetrator in history.

*Hitler's alpine domicile, "Berghof", on the Obersalzberg mountainside below the Hoher Göll massif.*

*Photo: Baumann*

# „Kill that dog!"

On a mild summer day in 1933, the freshly baked Chancellor Adolf Hitler showed himself before his house on the Obersalzberg to the columns of believers and gawkers. There an SA man („Storm Trooper") pressed furiously forward to such extent that Hitler's bodyguards grasped this brown uniformed man. During interrogation he gave a false name. He carried no identification. However, he did carry a cocked pistol in his trouser pocket. A lunatic or a mad assasin? The motives and fate of this man remained unknown.

What is known, on the contrary, is that since 1921 at least 40 plots against Hitler failed. Hitler always misinterpreted that as a hint of „Providence" to complete his great achievement.

Unfortunately, in 1937 providence didn't protect one of the most persistent and adventurous of the Hitler hunters, Swiss theology student Maurice Bavaud. He followed Hitler for five weeks throughout half of Germany, formally registered as a subtenant in five cities, and struck attention everywhere with his bad German. In Munich he bought a pistol along with ammunition and practiced shooting in a forest as well as on the Ammersee for so long that the noise caused a public disturbance.

Bavaud presented himself at the Munich Nazi party headquarters as a journalist and without any formality received a press seat on the stage of honor for the traditional 9 November festivities. At this procession - the commemoration of Hitler's failed coup in Munich on 9 November 1923 - Bavaud wanted to assassinate the Führer. But unfortunately Hitler marched out of range on the other side of the street.

Not annoyed, Bavaud followed the Nazi celebrity to Berchtesgaden. For days he reconnoitered the Obersalzberg and Hitler's routine. With the bungling, falsified letter of a French Nazi leader, Bavaud actually obtained admission to the Berghof. However, Hitler had already departed again. And so Bavaud decided (due to lack of

*Corporal Hitler in the First World War. In Austria he was certified as „unsuitable", whereupon he voluntarily registered himself for the German army in Bavaria. His regiment provided him for the first time in his life somewhat of a profession and the security of a group.*

Photo: Bavarian State Archives, Munich

money) to return home for the time being. Because he only had enough cash for a ticket to Munich, he travelled onward to Basel without a ticket. A conductor caught him and remanded him to the railroad police. Because he was a foreigner, they turned him over to the Gestapo, which very quickly pieced together Bavaud's incredible tale. Bavaud met his fate on the gallows after a secret trial.

Once, during World War II, Hitler came to speak of this „idealistically disposed assassin" and explained: There is no stopping such people, who set their life „carelessly at stake". Against

*As the new Reichs Chancellor in 1933, Hitler visibly enjoyed basking in the crowds on the Obersalzberg. However, the requirement to guarantee Hitlers security soon undermined such scenes. One wouldn't think that this apparently so affable man also explained at that time: „We must recapture a good conscience for cruelty (and thus) expunge the congeniality and evening cocktail bliss mentality of our people."*

*Photo: Baumann*

such assassins he was „saved by chance, not by police".

This had unnerved Chief of Staff General Franz Halder to such an extent that as early as 1939 (in the innermost circle of Hitler adversaries) he gruffly blurted: „Kill that dog!" However, nobody raised a hand against that man, who through incredible successes and the omnipotence of the Gestapo now strode to the peak of his career. Halder had constant access to Hitler and always took along a loaded pistol. But he never pulled it.

Chief of Military Intelligence Wilhelm Canaris, a key figure (later liquidated) in the plot against Hitler, characterized this hesitation: „We have nobody who throws the bomb to free our gene-

rals of their scruples". Scruples based on an oath of allegiance.

On 11 March 1944, chance once again led circumstances on the Obersalzberg. Captain Eberhard von Breitenbach was to accompany Field Marshals Busch, Jodl and Keitel as an orderly officer for a briefing with Hitler. In the left arm he carried Busch's file folder, in the trouser pocket a loaded Browning, and in his heart not the least of scruples about killing Hitler. However, Breitenbuch was surprisingly rejected by SS guards with the explanation that on this day no orderlies were allowed access. And so (with a pistol in his trouser pocket) the captain trembled through the end of the briefing amongst SS guards.

Four months to the day later, Hitler survived only due to a fully unaccustomed bungling by SS boss Heinrich Himmler. He missed a conference with the Führer and Luftwaffe Chief Hermann Göring on the Obersalzberg.

Colonel Count von Stauffenberg, Chief of Staff of the Replacement Army, was ordered to lecture on the declining reserves of the armed forces. These reserves were responsible for, among other things, „internal front" security; namely security against potential riots of 1.9 million prisoners of war or 5.7 million foreign forced laborers (together a quarter of the German work force).

Stauffenberg, long since the head of the conspirators against Hitler, carried in his attache case the official papers and a bomb into the Berghof. Because Himmler was unexpectedly missing, Stauffenberg asked the co-conspirators in Berlin (by telephone, in coded terms) if he should ignite the bomb. The answer was „no": they wanted to kill all three together. Thus it came to no more.

Stauffenberg's assassination attempt on 20 July 1944 at Hitler's Masurian „Wolfschanze" (Wolf's Lair) headquarters failed. The plot was exposed, and 2,000 Hitler adversaries were killed. Hitler only received the bullet from a weapon that he personally aimed while in the „Führer Bunker" under the ruins of the Reichs Chancellory on 30 April 1945. Thus ended a diabolic career which had begun with social descent.

Hitler was born in 1889 in Braunau, 80 kilometers to the north of Berchtesgaden, as the son of a customs official. In the secondary school he failed twice, at best received only poor grades, and dropped out of school as a 16 year old. Orphaned early, he ultimately lived in Vienna on a pension of between 246 and 315 euro (monetary value 2007). He passed the time with aimless loitering, amateurish painting, architectural sketches and enthusiasm for Wagner operas. In 1907, Hitler also failed the entrance examination for the Vienna Art Academy, which would have enabled him to graduate as an academic painter and architect. Since the path to that „pro-

*The 32 year old Hitler in 1921 as leader of the fledgling Nazi party. His self confident style as party chief: „I alone lead the Movement. Nobody places conditions upon me. I bear the total responsibility for everything." Nine years later he would announce: „I now consequently proclaim the right to political infallability for myself and my successors in the party leadership."* Photo: National Archives

fessional inclination" was now bridged, the eccentric, shy Hitler - always orderly but poorly dressed - refused any attempt at a „bread winning" profession. Therefore, until 1913, he dwelled in Vienna in meager rooms and shabby men's homes. Occasionally he sold watercolors. It once amused him in 1943, at the dinner table on Obersalzberg, that these amateurish works now sold on the market for the „mad" price of over 630 euro (monetary value 2007).

On the other hand, in Vienna Hitler indulged himself with zeal through racial theories, political pamphlets, weaponry and Richard Wagner

*Hitler appraised his success as well as the failure of about 40 assasination attempts as an indication of „Providence" that he was predestined to be the ruler of Europe. Because of this, the Nazi party agitated the public with propaganda images of the late Twenties like this Hitler quote as caption text: „Lord, bless our Struggle!"* Photo: State Archives

treatises over Germanics. Thus he also „discovered" the Jew as „the most decadent swine, that needs to be smashed". He began - quite characteristically for a social dropout in the Donau monarchy - to hate the Viennese „racial conglomerate and ethnic mixture"; he defined this metropolis of a multinational state as „the embodiment of incest".

In 1913 Hitler avoided the military draft by moving to Munich. There the disgrace fell upon him, that the Austrian consulate exposed him to the criminal investigation police as a deserter.

However, this passed without incident. Although he was required to undergo a military call up in Salzburg in February 1914, the doctor declared him „unsuitable for weapons and emergency service, too weak". (After the annexation of Austria in 1938, Hitler incited the Gestapo to the hunt for such documents and people who became acquainted with him as socially downgraded.)

Nevertheless, Hitler found employment after the outbreak of the First World War as a volunteer in a Bavarian regiment. Thus at age 25 this unskilled outsider received for the first time something of a professional task, a home and security among comrades - certainly with reservations, which suggest two remarkable deficiencies:

Only four (informal) friendships are known of Hitler (in his entire life he had only followers instead of friends); and there is no personally held letter from Hitler (he even wrote to his live-in companion Eva Braun in business-like fashion). According to the assessment of his superiors, Hitler only rose to the rank of lance corporal in World War I (1914-1918) due to „lack of corresponding leadership abilities". On the other hand, in combat he „....performed brilliantly. As a messenger he displayed cold-bloodedness and courage and was always ready to voluntarily relay messages, even through barrages under great life threatening conditions". Because of this - on the recommendation of the highly decorated Jewish regiment adjutant Hugo Gutmann - he received the very rare distinction (for that low rank) of being awarded the Iron Cross First Class. From the war Hitler culled the doctrine that indeed brutal self-assertion and not humanitarianism ensure survival.

Hitler - in the meantime blinded by poison gas - experienced the 1918 capitulation in a hospital; there he „decided to become a politician" because of indignation and disappointment. The chance arose later in Munich, where Hitler took care of office paperwork for his regiment and even propagated socialist ideas. There he impressed an officer as an eloquent and rousing debater among his comrades. And so he was prepared through democratically leftist cram courses for the political education of recruits. Among other things he was also skilled at „observation" of the assemblies that dozens of groups in revolutionary-correct Munich organized abundantly. Ultimately Hitler stumbled across the „German Workers Party" and became their seventh charter member. After his discharge from the army, Hitler seized the reins of the party. As a skilled tactician he maintained leadership, because he continually confronted his comrades with the choice between his unrestricted leadership or his resignation from the party.

This the meanwhile renamed „National Socialist German Worker's Party" (NSDAP) did not want to risk. Nonetheless, in beer tents and lounges, Hitler hooked many followers with vulgar word orgies against traitors, socialists, Jews and plutocrats, whom he threatened altogether with „pay back". This party was now a new home for the 32 year old Hitler. Of course, he still portrayed himself as an „author" or „painter"; however, the times were gone since a war comrade once described him in the following manner: „... like a tired stray dog, which looks for a master".

As a tactically and organizationally effective demagogue, Hitler employed political passion with the unprecedented gift of oratory and enthralled his listeners.

His never disguised purpose: „I can only lead the masses if I tear them away from their apathy. Only the fantasized masses become controllable. A mass which is apathetic and dull is the greatest danger for every community."

Hitler's „positive" characteristics corresponded to his favorite vocabulary, „ice cold": Will power, boldness, tenacity. Unequally colder were his negative characteristics: inconsiderate, vindictive, disloyal, cruel.

At that time, novelist Kurt Tucholsky assessed Hitler as concisely as he politically erred: „This man doesn't exist; he is only the noise which he creates."

Like Tucholsky, many clever people misjudged Hitler's monstruous aptitude for rhetoric mastery so long, until it was too late: After the „Seizure of Power" on 30 January 1933, Hitler produced the theatricals of processions and military power with unscrupulous tactical agility. However, East Europe as a „German Living Space" as well antisemitism, antimarxism and a Darwinian ideological struggle („Survival of the Fittest") remained constant dimensions in his narrow field of political vision. These attitudes communicated world domination by the German master race.

Hitler actually was reduced by the years of economic upswing from 1924-1929 to a noisy nonentity. The chances for his demagogic and organizational talent came during times of economic bad weather - in the devastating inflation after the First World War and during the international economic crisis which set millions of unemployed on the street after 1929. Both times people asked about those guilty for the misery - and Hitler delivered them: Jews, war profiteers, socialists, communists. Both times people demanded work and bread - Hitler promised them both. In 1945, only a scene of devastation remained.

*„We will march on, until everything falls to pieces, because today Germany belongs to us - and tomor-row the entire World". History ordained other than that which the beloved marching song proclaimed: Hitler's Berghof in May of 1945.*

*Pension „Moritz". Hitler arrived here in 1923 during his first visit to Berchtesgaden and was enraptured with the magnificent panorama. This house, later renamed „Platterhof", was at that time one of six comfortable inns on the touristically well-known Obersalzberg. A childrens sanitarium and 11 villas of noble citizens were also located on the mountainside. Among others of fame, Freud and Brahms spent vacations at the „Moritz". In 1936, the Nazis requisitioned the „Platterhof" for a ridiculously low price and rebuilt it as a „People's Hotel". This later withstood the 1945 bombing raid and was maintained by the American military as „Hotel General Walker" until 1995.*     Photo: Archive Dr. Feulner

*Until 1936 the small road from Berchtesgaden to Obersalzberg served in winter as a „timber road", sled run and downhill ski run. This ultimately and abruptly ceased due to the large scale, frenzied expansion and closure of the „Führer Area" to the public.*     Photo: Archive Dr. Feulner

*At the end of the Twenties, construction of a cog wheel train from Berchtesgaden was considered in order to facilitate access to the Obersalzberg for skiers. However, preliminary cost estimates led to selection of a less expensive variation — „Caterpillar tracked vehicles", like those utilized in alpine pass elevations in Austria and Switzerland. Such a vehicle had 10 passenger seats, and, with 50 horsepower, could propel at speeds up to 55 km/hr on level terrain, while it was capable of climbing steep grades of up to 40 percent. The excursion up the Obersalzberg mountainside - 400 height meters and 4 kilometers - lasted 30 minutes and cost (in 2007 monetary value) a haughty 16 euro!*   Photo: Archive Dr. Feulner

# „Herr Wolf" appears

„This is my young friend Herr Wolf". So presented houseguest Dr. Hoffmann a man to the owners of pension „Moritz" (later „Hotel Platterhof") on the Obersalzberg one April morning in 1923. This man had come to Berchtesgaden for the first time the day before, ascended the Obersalzberg by night, and had been housed by Dr. Hoffmann in a room. On this radiant mor-

*A parade of the motley arrayed „Storm Troopers" (SA) at a Nazi rally in 1923. In the beginning, the SA provided security for Hitler's public appearances. But very soon the SA developed itself into a feared brawling force that brutally dispersed the events of other parties and blatantly intimidated people not in favor of Hitler. Only later did the SS „Security Detachment" emerge from the ranks of the SA. They were responsible for Hitler's personal safety. The rise of the SS began in 1934 when Hitler - under the pretense of an SA conspiracy - liquidated any competition within the party. Thereafter the SA faded into a meaningless entity.*                    *Photo: State Archive*

*Idyllic Haus Wachenfeld in a dream location on the Obersalzberg. Eventually, Hitler acquired this house, and later, through immense effort, expanded it to form a sort of second seat of government that was renamed „Berghof" (meaning, „Estate on the Mountain"). Notice the kitchen garden in front of the house and the bleached laundry in the meadow. At right in the photo: Hitler on the way to his auto.*

ning Herr Wolf assessed the panorama from this pension above the Berchtesgadener Land as „splendid, wonderful, indescribable".

Exactly because of this location prominent people had long since valued „House Moritz". For instance, the summer before Viennese professor Sigmund Freud had vacationed with his family here and had debated with Viennese doctor and poet Arthur Schnitzler about the marital problems of Viennese composer Gustav Mahler.

Dr. Hoffmann invited Herr Wolf from Austria to the „Türkenwirt" (five minutes by foot below the „Moritz") for „a proper goulash". There he introduced his friend once again as „Herr Wolf". It visibly troubled Herr Wolf that the proprietors evidently knew the „Doctor" well. However the „Doctor" soothed: „Up here there are no traitors!"

Behind the alias Dr. Hoffmann hid none other than Dr. Dietrich Eckart: a nationally renowned author with an aggressively caustic pen, Bohemian, friend of liquor, rough antisemite, translator of Ibsen, National Socialist of the first hour, chief editor of the Nazi newspaper „National Observer" and, as a witty thinker, valued in Munich's best circles.

The police sought Eckart once again because of vulgar defamation. This time Eckart had slandered the social democratic Reichs President Friedrich Ebert. However, influential like-minded friends had smuggled Eckart in a requisitioned military car from Munich out to a „costly hiding place" in Berchtesgaden - to the „Moritz". If necessary, it would only be a cat's leap from there across the border into Austria.

Herr Wolf - long since known to the police because of unrestrained propaganda against the state - was a year previously sentenced to six weeks imprisonment after a bungling „revolutionary action" along with breach of the peace in Mu-

14

nich. He had also come incognito to visit Eckart on the Obersalzberg. This man was none other than Adolf Hitler. He venerated the well educated and 21 year older Eckart as an intellectual mentor and as a master of well-honed manners. In January 1941, Hitler - during his nightly fireplace chats - fondly related details of his first visit to Obersalzberg: The guests in the pension called him „Wolf". Nobody recognized him, because no photos of him had yet appeared in the newspapers. „That was for me the most beautiful time!" That incognito certainly ended in Berchtesgaden a few days later. Hitler was billed as guest speaker for the 1923 „German Day". Excitement reigned in the pension up above, be-

cause nearly 50 guests absolutely wanted to see Hitler;s appearance. Therefore the meal was even scheduled earlier. As Hitler then appeared at the ceremony, he experienced „the craziest: My entire pension sat before me!" Certainly afterwards „life in the pension for me was destroyed, because all of those who had previously scolded about me now felt embarrassed".

Henceforth Hitler came again and again to Berchtesgaden, especially for relaxation after stressful journeys to party events throughout Germany or for the preparation of large campaigns. He later also confessed to his table companions: „For me the Obersalzberg became something quite wonderful. I completely fell in

*A famous photo of Hitler's imprisonment in Landsberg. Because of his bloody coup attempt on 9 November 1923 in Munich, Hitler was sentenced to five years imprisonment, but was released after only nine months. Influential friends ensured for a comfortable incarceration. Thus Hitler (left) could optionally receive visitors and dictate the programmatic book „Mein Kampf" („My Struggle") to his secretary Rudolf Hess (second from right) for typing.* Photo: State Archives

love with this landscape. Here were the most beautiful times of my life. My great plans have emerged here."

However, a sharp break in Hitler's course followed.

On 9 November 1923, Hitler - with his already proven SA brown brigade („Storm Troopers") and other small nationalistic groups - risked the „National Uprising" in Munich against the Bavarian government. But the attempted coup with its arrogant „March to the Field Marshall Memorial" ended with a shootout and a fiasco shortly before its goal due to a military barricade: 14 Hitler loyalists and three policemen were killed; however, the marching column disintegrated in wild flight.

Hitler also took flight, although he was certainly hindered by a painful arm (which he had dislocated after stumbling). He hid with acquaintances 50 km south Munich. There his shoulder was treated and friends feverishly tried to find a car for an escape via Berchtesgaden and the Obersalzberg into Austria. The police, however, were faster and apprehended Hitler.

Hitler cleverly manipulated the subsequent high treason trial into a platform for political propaganda. Because the judges allowed this, Hitler came away quite cheaply with only five years imprisonment. The state proved itself even more generous after a harsh Nazi election defeat: after only nine months of unusually comfortable imprisonment - during which Hitler had dictated the programmatically confusing book „Mein Kampf" to his secretary Rudolf Hess - he was released.

Afterwards, however, the failed rebel jeered: „Landsberg was my university at public expense. I recognized the accuracy of my views and became content considering the whole contradictory, hypocritical Knowledge of the professors and the university priests altogether. In the end, volition is more than knowledge."

From this arrogant self-image a poorly educated Hitler concocted his claim to the unrestricted Führer Principle in party and state: „I lead (the party) alone, and nobody places conditions upon

me, as long as I personally carry the total responsibility for everything."

Thus the Nazi party received their „Blood Christening" that 9 November 1923: a reason to produce their martyrs and annual festivals, which were exceeded only by every Nürnberg „Reichsparteitag" (Party conventions) in emotionalism and expense. At that time, Hitler found more time for Berchtesgaden than was necessary. Because of his rhetorical excesses and the atrocities of the SA, again once a ban on speaking had literally disarmed him politically. Additionally, the Damocles sword of expulsion as an undesirable foreigner still hung unpleasantly over Hitler. Despite his emigration to Munich in 1913, Hitler had remained Austrian - even as a volunteer in the German army. In 1922 the Bavarian Interior Ministry considered expelling this notorious trouble maker and demagogic agitator to Austria. However, it never did get around to it; of all parties, specifically the SPD (Social Democrats) intervened with a sharp objection against such an injury of democratic principles. As thanks, Hitler fought the SPD his life long with a blood oath.

Indeed, Hitler now emphatically pursued his expatriation from Austria with the assertion that he be „for the purpose of acquisition of German citizenship excluded from the bond of state". The authorities in Linz approved this step for a fee of 23 euro (monetary value 2007). This trifle anecdote made world history like Hitler's failure of the entrance examination at the Vienna Art Academy: Without German citizenship the active and passive right to vote in Germany would have been denied.

After imprisonment in Landsberg, Hitler rented a room at the Berchtesgadener „Deutschen Haus" and there wrote the second part of „Mein Kampf". In these evidently unencumbered days, the meanwhile 36 year old man experienced his first love - with a minor. Across from the hotel, the two daughters of Berchtesgaden SPD co-founder Reiter operated a fashion shop. With the younger sister, 17 year old Mitzi, Hitler so successfully made advances (while walking his dog

*Hitler's living room in the old Haus Wachenfeld. The porcelain furnace, paneling, carpets and seating booth in the flat bay windows convey simple comforts. The highly modern radio in the left corner is noteworthy.*

„Wolf" in the public park) that Mitzi attempted suicide in 1927 from jealousy. As Hitler then turned to other women, Mitzi ultimately found her luck with a prominent Nazi.

While relating to the key developments of that time, Hitler later told his fireside companions: Daily he hiked up to the Obersalzberg. „Then I hear from somebody that „Haus Wachenfeld" is for rent. There can't be anything more beautiful than that, I said to myself."

This simple house belonged to the widow of Buxtehude leather producer Winter and was called „Wachenfeld" (after the maiden name of the 84 year old lady). Hitler hurried posthaste to Frau Winter: „I heard that you want to rent." Winter: „You are Herr Hitler? We also belong to you. We are party members!" Hitler:" That's

wonderful, can I rent the whole house the entire year? What does it cost? „ Winter: „Well, I don't know whether it's too much for you. 324 euro per month (monetary value 2007)." Hitler: „ Immediately! And in case you want to sell, a pre-sale agreement for me." The old lady thereupon: „You relieve us of a colossal chore! We can't do anything with this house."

Hitler bore the 3.890 euro yearly rent easily. Because already in the first year (1925) „Mein Kampf" earned him at least 13.500 euro (monetary value 2007), and sales soared due to the growing number of party members.

And so Hitler now invited his widowed half-sister Angela Raubal from Vienna to run the household at „Haus Wachenfeld". She came, „and we moved in immediately. It was so wonderful!

The first Christmas up there was splendid." Hitler procured two more German shepherds so that Angela felt secure.

Months later chance again led circumstances - Hitler arrived in Buxtehude (of all days) on the day after after the burning of the Winter leather factory to discuss the reconstruction and perhaps also the purchase of „Haus Wachenfeld". According to Hitler's description, Frau Winter was perplexed: „I consider it as a luck that you have come today (after the burning). You know, there is still justice." (Hitler's later commentary: „The factory had been bartered away during the days of inflation to two Jews.") Then the daughter turned to her mother: „Herr Hitler would like to buy the house on the mountain." Winter: „Today! Because it's such a lucky day, I'm in agreement". However, it took until 26 July 1933 before the house passed over to Hitler's possession (for barely 135.000 euro, monetary value 2007) and advanced to the scene of historical meaning.

Hitler's architect Albert Speer so described this house shortly before the reconstruction: „Small, comfortable wooden house with an overhanging roof and five modest rooms. The furniture originated from old German folkloric style and gave the impression of a comfortable middle class lifestyle. A gilded cage with a canary, a cactus and a rubber plant further strengthened this impression".

And on the other hand, Hitler's Foreign Press Secretary Ernst („Putzi") Hanfstaengl recollected: „The study had a small desk and a few simple bookshelves, surprisingly the majority of them filled with Wild West novels by Karl May."

*The official party text to this photo of Hitler taking a break reads: „A man of no pretensions. In a few hours ten thousand will enthusiastically exult him." The culinary simplicity of the vegetarian and teetotaler Hitler was proverbial. These traits were later portrayed by the propaganda during harsh war times as exemplary behavior. It is hard to believe that this man uttered the following sentence: „Two things enable one to unify people: common ideals and common trickery."*     Photo: State Archives

# Ten Square Kilometers: „Führer Area"

The petty bourgeois idyll of „Haus Wachenfeld" was no longer sufficient for Chancellor Hitler. Immediatedly after the purchase in1933, the house received a terrace, a winter garden and an expanded garage. In 1935-36, Munich architect Alois Degano subsequently enlarged „Wachenfeld" by four times the original area (based on Hitler sketches) into the pseudoalpin, manorial „Berghof" (with 30 rooms). The technical gem was an 8 by 4 m large retracting window in the lobby, which revealed a view of the grandiose panorama between the Hochkalter mountain and Salzburg.

The Führer easily financed construction costs from his own pocket. He declared an income of 3.8 million euro (monetary value 2007) to the treasury in 1933. In addition, he received a chancellor's salary of about 189,000 euro (monetary value 2007).

Hitler transformed the Obersalzberg into a pilgrimage site for comrades and gawkers, and thus the bed capacity of the region rose from 4,323 in1933 to 10,540 in 1934. People were led in droves before „Wachenfeld". If the Führer had time, he very gladly displayed himself in civilian attire before the hand shakers and cameras. However, if more important tasks or the need for rest claimed his time, then the masses had to satiate themselves (out of earshot) with a glimpse of Hitler's domicile. And the guards strictly enforced the prohibition that „any movement of the People's Chancellor be constantly observed through binoculars".

Even in Salzburg the police intervened against people who observed the Obersalzberg from the fortress or hills with telescopes: This disturbs the Führer's privacy.

The Idyll on the Obersalzberg had thoroughly withstood the previously modest touristic expansion because of the construction of „Pension Moritz" in 1877. Because they were attracted by the scenery and healthy mountain climate, cultural luminaries (among them Clara Schumann

*From 1933 onwards Hitler thoroughly purged everyone of the desire for caricature and opposition through use of the Gestapo and concentration camps. During the World Depression crisis after 1929, Hitler promised the growing army of unemployed the blue heavens. This placard pertains to that regard. After 1941 things nonetheless became much more severe.*　　*Photo: State Archives*

and Johannes Brahms) ascended the Obersalzberg. That now inevitably changed, because (according to the Nazi party plans) the Obersalzberg was destined to remain „in the forseeable future a pilgrimage destination for the German people" and also functioned as a quasi second seat of government, vacation home and pleasure palace.

Already in the summer of 1933, the „Türke" (meanwhile molted from a tavern into a hotel) was forced to close because of a much too slight „respectability distance" of 100 meters from the Berghof. However, the owner - a harmless party member from the earliest brown days - was the victim of an evil defamation and was subsequently expropriated without compensation. Because of its proximity to the Berghof, the house was initially adapted for the SS guard detachment and later for the Nazi Secret Service.

The „Führer Area" was surrounded by a 3 km long fence, which guests occasionally ridiculed as an open air enclosure for political carnivores. It was only accessible through two guarded gates and was later doubly secured through an extensive, almost 10 km long fence.

Whatever furthermore happened on the Obersalzberg danced to Martin Bormann's tune. Hitler's almighty secretary procured a gigantic, inexhaustible financial source for the needs of Hitler and the Party itself through the annual „Führer Donation from German Industry". Up until 1937 he snatched up nearly 10 square kilometers of property on the Obersalzberg through sugar-loafing and dire threats against stubborn hold-outs („....denial can only be answered with your admission into the Dachau Concentration Camp....") and paid roughly 22,5 million euro (monetary value 2007).

Thus 51 properties belonging to 400 long established Obersalzberg residents yielded to an inconsiderate building boom, which transformed this magnificent landscape by 1944 into a huge construction site. Even during the war, an average of 3,000 workers toiled here - predominantly Italians, but also „labor conscripted" Czechs, Poles and Ukrainians. Though the heavy industry suffered from a substantial lack of laborers, Bormann nonetheless trampled an entire municipality through somewhat extreme terrain with these labor brigades.

Among other things which emerged: a gigantic parade ground with underground shooting range, two large troop barracks (for a 350 man SS detachment), a large motor pool with garage, a theater & film hall for 2,000 people (to entertain the entire Obersalzberg work force), a hotel (along with its own employee quarters) for Hitler's guests, an administrative center, a kindergarten, a permanent architecture display, an agra-

*Enthusiasm for the Führer (in the highly modern Mercedes next to the driver) on the Obersalzberg: Hitler departing along the steep gravel road down to Berchtesgaden. From this man stems the brutal proclamation: „Now there is no compassion. Whoever stands in our way will be annihilated."*

*Photo: State Archives*

*The lobby in the Kehlsteinhaus („Eagle's Nest") featured a collection of the most carefully selected building materials and furnishings. Amidst this lofty ambience the Führer acknowledged in 1940: „Treaties are merely to be maintained as long as they suit a purpose." During his reign Hitler broke no less than 84 international treaties.*                                                                                                          *Photo: Baumann*

rian estate (with 80 oxen, 100 pigs and 60 Haflinger breeding studs), a huge 110 by 26 meter greenhouse (today a concrete parking lot beside the Kehlstein bus station), and an administration facility. The still existing settlements Hintereck, Klaushöhe and Buchenhöhe (along with school, kindergarten, tavern, business and sports halls) were necessary to accommodate the growing numbers of employees.

A dense network of underground telephone lines (a strategically ultra-modern undertaking) throughout the Obersalzberg served the needs of the brown prominents wherever and whenever the desire arose.

Wherever dwellings were not erected, heavy truck traffic rumbled day and night through the quiet mountain landscape - as long as the convalescing Führer was not in residence. Meanwhile, a road network totalling 42.1 km was thrust upon this age old farming countryside. All together, this incessant 24 hour a day energy consumption devoured electricity to such an ex-

tent that - despite the addition of a Berchtesgaden county hydroelectric plant in 1936 and a heating plant (500 kilowatt diesel driven) - not enough electricity was available! In addition, connecting electricity cable to the rest of Bavaria by way of Reichenhall was not possible, because this town also suffered a chronic dearth of electricity. Therefore, immediately after the annexation of Austria in 1938, the municipal electric plant for the city of Salzburg provided energy for Obersalzberg.

In honor of Hitler's 49th birthday in 1938, Bormann dreamed up something truly extraordinary: A house on the 1834 m high Kehlstein mountain, connected through a 6.4 km long, breathtaking alpine road - hewn out of solid rock and adjoined for the final 124 height meters through an elevator inside the mountain! A pump system supplied water up 700 height meters from the lower „Scharitzkehlalm". The huge, pompous facilities on the Kehlstein (which were meant to impress prominent guests) devoured roughly

162 million euro (monetary value 2007), but nevertheless failed their purpose. Hitler couldn't withstand heights and only visited this house a few times. Fortunately, today's tourists profit from this extraordinarily-perched lookout.

What is referred to today as „Eagle's Nest" or „Tea House" - and at the end of the war even considered the central command of the Potemkin-like „Alpine Fortress" - owes its name to the „D" abbreviation for „diplomacy" and representation.

Only this „D-House" on the Kehlstein outlasted undamaged Hitlers demise. However, of the real „Tea House" - a pavilion on the „Mooslahnerkopf" visited almost daily by Hitler - nothing more remains except for the remnants of a small terrace. The 20 minute walk from the Berghof to this pavillion led over the fields of the „Gutshof" estate. Today, an exceptionally beautiful golf course is situated here.

The „Gutshof" - an economic delicacy of the „Führer Area" - was located slightly beneath the Berghof. Martin Bormann (a semi-skilled farmer) wanted to impress his boss Hitler and „ensure the nourishment of the Führer" - of course, „strictly according to private sector points of view". In practice it looked this: „Gutshof" received potatos from a synchronized „Gutshof" in the northern German state of Mecklenburg and shipped these in abundance, wherever the current Führer headquarters rotated: between Winniza (Ukraine), „Wolfsschanze" (Masuria) or the Palatinate. On the contrary, the grain for hundreds of grain beds and feeding troughs which Hitler had placed throughout the Obersalzberg came from the Ukraine (where masses of people starved). However, thanks to Bormann's inexhaustible slush fund, „Gutshof" always fared well. Nevertheless, Hitler once read the bottom line financial statements of this operation and then commented sarcastically: „Outstanding! A liter of milk costs me at most 14,40 euro (monetary value 2007). For that price the local mountain farmers could have delivered the twentyfold quantity."

Hitler granted only three „Chosen" the privile-

*A tenacious misunderstanding: The Kehlsteinhaus (above) was referred to as „Tea House" (and also „Eagle's Nest"); however, the real „Tea House" (below) stood on the Mooslahnerkopf about 20 minutes by foot away from Hitler's Berghof along the perimeter of today's golf course. The ruins of the platform to the left of the „Tea House" remain today. The parking lot directly under the Kehlsteinhaus is noticeable. From there an elevator leads upwards to the „Eagle's Nest".* Photo: Baumann

ge of settling on the Obersalzberg. First came the irreplaceable secretary Martin Bormann, the gray eminence of the brown empire. Number two was the corpulent Reichs Marshall Hermann Göring, a highly decorated combat pilot in World War I and early Hitler adherent who organized the air force and trimmed the German economy on a war course.

The young architect Albert Speer assumed a special role. His work enthused Hitler to such an extent that he arranged a generous studio for him on the Obersalzberg. This studio (as well as Speer's apartment house) consisted of squared stone blocks and attests today as an architectural style example of that time. It is located across the street from „Gutshof" amidst a meadow. Speer later advanced to Minister of Armaments. On the other hand, Foreign Secretary Joachim von Ribbentrop amused himself with „Schloß Fuschl", a magical idyll along the lake of the same name in Austria's Salzkammergut region. From here, Ribbentrop managed his noble guest houses along the approaches to Obersalzberg: The elegant „Schloß Klessheim" near Salzburg and the exclusive „Österreichischer Hof" in the Mozart city.

When the civilian buildings on the Obersalzberg stood finished, military security measures began in 1943 due to the impression of increased allied bombing raids. Five kilometers of tunnels and 4,000 square meters of luxurious living space were built inside the mountain. Everything was equipped with air-conditioning, kitchens, separate water supply, marble tiles, parquet floors, gas filters, operating rooms, rooms for pet dogs and machine gun positions.

In addition, 10 air defense batteries with 54 guns were installed (up to 2,000 SS men served duty), as well as 270 instruments for artificially covering the Berchtesgaden valley basin with fog during air raid warnings. This fog could be produced in 20 to 30 minutes (depending on humidity) by 640 battle-unsuitable, but specially trained soldiers.

Beginning in 1944, air raids on targets in Bavaria and Austria increased. Thus Hitler had to re-

*A large sports field is situated among trees west of the Hintereck (bus stop, cafe) on the Obersalzberg. This former exercise field of the SS guard detachment was tunneled after a huge effort. Thus the SS received an underground shooting range and didn't disturb Hitler's tranquility. A barracks together with a sports hall for the SS and a large garage stood around the field. This is why tens of thousands of cubic meters of earth were moved, and consistently sliding terrain was fortified with concrete constructions. The horrendous costs were borne by German industry due to the Bormann-inspired yearly „Führer Donation".* Photo: Baumann

gularly seek air raid shelter. Nevertheless, before 25 April 1945, no bomb fell on the Obersalzberg; the allies wanted to capture Hitler alive. On the other hand, in 1944 the always studiously busy Bormann blocked the south-eastern tip of Bavaria and the adjacent state of Salzburg against the influx of bombed out national and party officials in order to avoid providing any additional incentives for the Allied bomber fleets.

Altogether Hitler and Bormann spent a minimum of 1.5 billion euro (monetary value 2007) in land acquisition, buildings, and immense changes, as well as military security of difficult terrain and luxurious designs on the Obersalzberg. Of all this, after the only Allied bombing raid on 25 April 1945 (with 373 airplanes and 1,232 tons of bombs) only ruins remained.

Hermann Göring emerged from his deep bunker into this domain of ruins. On Hitler's 56th birthday (20 April), Göring had himself excused from the Berlin Reichs Chancellory in order to complete „most urgent tasks in Southern Germany". And on 23 April, while on the Obersalzberg, he learned of Hitler's decision that the Führer will personally take over the defense of Berlin and will shoot himself in the last moment. Hitler's reasoning: „ I can not thereby lead, if I

*Hitler inspects the progress of the construction work on the Obersalzberg. His secretary Bormann organized this extravagant construction frenzy with full brutality: Even in the worst times of war, Bormann - until the end of 1944 - utilized thousands of workers on the Obersalzberg, as well as the best in building materials, furnishings and machines. Millions of bombing victims had no inkling of this, because Germany lay under the strictest censorship. It is not without reason that Hitler boasted of his Nazi party: „ ... the only party that has thoroughly subdued democratic thoughts."*                    Photo: Baumann

*The pompous house on the Kehlstein peak and a panorama road up to the observation point are counted amongst the most lavish projects in Bormann's construction program. This surprise gift for Hitler's 49th birthday was nevertheless rarely utilized, because the recipient could not bear heights. However, this facility primarily served a purpose to impress prominent guests. This photo from the Kehlstein road shows a rarity: A prewar VW convertible from Hitler's motor pool on the Obersalzberg.*   Photo: Baumann

sit somewhere on a mountain. I did not come to the World merely to defend only my Berghof." Thus Göring smelled the chance for his last great appearance. He inquired telegraphically in Berlin, whether now, since the Führer was incapable of acting, the law of 1941 took effect (which would make Göring Hitler's successor). Hitler raged, cursed Göring as a lazy sluggard, failure, morphine addict, unprecedented corruptionist, and degraded him from all offices. Bormann taunted for so long, until Hitler also expelled Göring from the party because of high treason. Whereupon Bormann directed the SS on the Obersalzberg to arrest Göring and shoot him to death - „after our death" (in Berlin).

The SS hesitated, placed Göring under „honorable house arrest" and shipped him (after the luckily-endured bombing raid) to his palatial mansion at Mauterndorf in the state of Salzburg. After Hitler's suicide (30 April), Göring headed westward for „negotiations" with Allied Supreme Commander Eisenhower. However this political dream excursion ended abruptly in Kitzbühel with imprisonment by the Americans. Göring had to answer for himself in Nuremberg as a capital war criminal, and was condemned to death at the gallows. He committed suicide (by taking potassium cyanide) two hours before the appointed execution on the night of 16 October 1946.

After the heavy bombing raid on the Obersalzberg, the SS allowed the local population to plunder the ruins. On the evening of 4 May 1945, US troops occupied the Obersalzberg. And in 1952 the last remnants of the „Führer Area" were demolished. Only the „Platterhof" and the adjacent ruins of the employee quarters remained. The occasionally recognizable ruins of foundation blocks of the former splendor was long since overgrown by forest and shrubbery.

Thus an apprehension was eliminated. Hitler had once expressed to his fireplace companions in 1943, on the eve of his 54th Birthday: It would be dreadful if the Berghof would become a museum after his death, whereby tourist guides would explain: „Here he always had breakfast." It would be better if the entire Berghof ignited as a „magnificent pyre" in flames.

*The national wealth was carelessly squandered on this tiny guard house above the large garage facility. Because Bormann insisted that it must stand on the valley side of the road, it was necessary to set a 20 meter deep concrete foundation through the steep mountain slope into solid boulders. Thus a 9,900 euro (2007 value) guard post received an 360,000 euro concrete base.*    Photo: Baumann

# Hitler's Path to War

Germany's path to a totalitarian, despotic government and into World War II began on 3 February 1933. This was only four days after Hitler had formed a coalition on 30 January with disputing parties and had been appointed Chancellor by Reichs President Hindenburg. The Nazi jargon heroicized this process as „Seizure of Power Day".

On that 3 February Hitler addressed the assembled military leadership in a two-hour speech and demanded that the rearmament of Germany is the first requirement. Therefore that „cancerous ulcer, democracy" must be eradicateed. As soon as Germany would then be mighty again, the „conquest of new living space in the East and its indiscriminate Germanization" would begin.

Then it went blow by blow. On 22 February 1933 an auxiliary police was formed from the 50,000 men of the SA and the SS. This force was an armed party army with the mandate to club down any opposition. In order that this also function radically, the infamous „Emergency Decree for the Protection of People and State" of 27 February 1933 replaced the constitutional state through a permanent state of emergency. (The Reichstag (Parliament) arson of the previous night provided a welcomed pretense.)

This most important of all Third Reich laws delivered Hitler's dictatorship the apparent authority of legal foundation. It cancelled all basic rights and authorized the police to arrest „also outside legal boundaries", to impose unrestricted prison terms, and to deprive the arrested of legal recourse.

The provisional Munich Chief of Police, SS boss Heinrich Himmler, didn't allow this opportunity to escape. On 20 March 1933, he opened the first „protective custody camp" for 5,000 people at Dachau - the first concentration camp, where up until 1945 206,000 prisoners were tormented and 32,000 were killed.

*This propaganda photo was taken during October 1931 in Braunschweig. At that time Hitler had many reasons for a good mood. Because in Braunschweig it was finally possible for him to receive German citizenship, which was essential for his political ambitions. Therefore he recited the so-called „Legality Oath": He wanted to achieve power only by democratic means.* Photo: State Archives

Hitler placed great value on the appearance of legality. He thus blackmailed the Parliament (amidst the climate of brown terror) on 21 March 1933 to accept both the „Malicie Act" (legalizing terror against any opposition) and two days later the „Enabling Act" - in end effect the suicide of German democracy. Henceforth, the government „was permitted „ to decree laws which „deviate from the constitution", and to dissolve other political parties for the purpose of „security of the Party and

**Adolf Hitler: „Im Kampf haben wir einst das Deutsche Reich erobert,**
und im Kampf werden wir es erhalten und bewahren." Der Führer sprach am Tage des 15jährigen Bestehens der
zweitältesten Ortsgruppe der NSDAP. in Rosenheim. Nie kann die kleine Schar der Zweifler und Spötter der Bewegung
etwas anhaben, der Gedanke an eine Fortsetzung des Kampfes aber wird ihnen noch völlig vergehen. Im Bild: Der
Führer beim Deutschlandlied inmitten alter Kämpfer auf dem Max-Joseph-Platz.

*Hitler in classic Führer pose. The original photo text reads: „In struggle we once conquered the German empire, and in struggle we will maintain and protect it." Hitler came to power through a legal coalition. But he used his power for massive intimidation in order to destroy democracy - according to stringent legal formalities. Accordingly, Hitler's cynical commentary from 30 January 1941: „I have conquered Democracy through its own madness!"*

*Photo: State Archives*

state unit" (December 1933). This legally declared the NSDAP as the official party, and subjected all media to comprehensive censorship.

Therefore Hitler quite legally obtained his terrorist, despotic government: „The basis of the interpretation of all legal sources is the National Socialist world view." Their explanation, however, lay exclusively with the leader.

On 2 May 1933, unions and employee associations were replaced through the „German Workers Front", whereby the Gestapo enforced a social harmony. Therefore „managers"

(enterpreneurs) - for the higher welfare of the Third Reich - could thus increase daily working hours from eight up to 12 hours without supplementary pay.

Uncontested is the fact that Hitler, within four years, removed nearly 6 million unemployed from the streets. This international propaganda list certainly presupposed that the totalitarian regime transformed the armaments industry (through immense tasking) into the motor of the economy. In the years 1933-39, no less than a sixth of German internal production was attributed to armaments.

Naturally the industry expanded without precedent, especially since rigorous wage and price freezes curbed consumption in favor of armaments.

Hitler wanted to make Germany strong, but he did not want to make the Germans rich. Consequently, production of consumer goods in 1938 was below the level of 1928; and 54 percent of the Germans in 1938 lived on a miserable 300 euro (monetary value 2007) or less per month. However the people had work again, and that weighed more heavily than a party dictatorship which „only" straightened-up dissenters, other races and the conspicuously rebellious left wing intellectuals. Therefore nobody dared to break the spell of the propaganda-popular „Reichs autobahn". It provided work for over 150,000 people - including suppliers and the „Reichsarbeits-

dienst" (a miserably paid, quasi-paramilitary labor service.)

Meanwhile, on the Obersalzberg, the affable child-stroking, dog-loving Hitler openly displayed his unusual style of loafing to such an extent that the philosopher Oswald Spengler sarcastically noted: the Third Reich means „the unemployed being organized by the lazy". And this organization steered a course straight toward war, as Hitler's instructions for the initial four year plan attest: „1. In four years the German army must be deployable. 2. In four years the German economy must be capable of war." And on 5 November 1937, Hitler proclaimed to the leaders of the armed forces his „irrevocable decision" to engage in war: Because the living space of the German people is not to be won peacefully, only force remains.

*One of the first autobahns built was the section from Munich towards Salzburg. Thus Hitler achieved effective propaganda in nearby Austria, where unemployment in the Thirties swelled to 26 percent. „Work on autobahn construction" was an electrifying slogan in Austria. This double photo depicts Hitler leading an auto column during the opening of 26 kilometers from Munich eastwards.* Photo: State Archives

*Before Hitler was appointed Reichs Chancellor in 1933, he gladly wore folkloric costumes in order to appear more appealing to the indigenous population. Thus it didn't disturb him in the least if he were ridiculed because of such clothing. On the contrary, he steadfastly avoided slipping into bathing trunks. He considered that improper for a politician - and referred to photos that depicted the somewhat corpulent first German Reichs President Friedrich Ebert in a swimsuit.*

In the summer of 1940, Hitler reached the zenith of his power: He drove as victor through Paris and celebrated his last triumphal procession through Berlin. Notwithstanding his methods - he had fulfilled all his programmatic promises.

Hitler had torn up the foolish „Dictate of Versailles", with which the victors of 1918 had not only placed all war guilt on Germany, but also the burden of immense reparations and the inability for military defense. The victors additionally committed the devastating folly, neither to disempower nor to durably integrate the outlawed Germany into Europe. Therefore „Versailles" bequeathed a dangerous vacuum in the center of Europe.

Hitler also deducted that the predominantly socialist „November criminals" had set in gear the 1918 democratic revolution within the German hinterland, and thus fed the legend that a „stab in the back" brought the undefeated German army to defeat.

In 1934, after the bloody party purge, he had achieved all power in Germany - there was absolutely nothing more to be gotten.

He had cancelled the „disgrace of Versailles" with the introduction of compulsory military service (forbidden by the „Versailles Treaty") and with the invasion of the demilitarized Rhineland.

Unpunished, he had violently led Austria and the Sudetenland „home into the Reich", and then smashed the rest of Czechoslovakia.

He had „bullied" the world and thus achieved what imperial Germany in World War I strove for in vain: The unassailable dominance of power in Europe.

These are indisputable achievements, as long as one accepts the immorality that the purpose justifies the means. Now, however, Hitler „played for keeps", as his first defeat loomed in May of 1941: Militarily inferior Britain had won the since August 1940 raging „Air Battle over England", because their incredibly underestimated fighter planes were superior to the highly praised German air force.

Without air domination over England, however, „Operation Sea Lion" came to pass:

The invasion of England. Not once did Hitler suspect how deeply the Britons already were able to look at his cards. They had cracked all the German codes with their „Ultra" system, and with the first radars directed their fighter squadrons unerringly against Hitler's bomber fleets.

In this thoroughly uncomfortable situation the violence-proned Hitler also revealed himself as a political bungler: „Wars have always been ended only through the destruction of the adversary. Anyone who thinks differently is irresponsible."

But what now, since England had escaped destruction and remained the unassailable rival, who absolutely did not have to seek peace with Hitler? Then Hitler committed his first cardinal mistake: He offered Poland and France no honorable peace. Should that have come into existence in 1940, then what should London have still fought for?

Therefore Hitler also groped into his second cardinal mistake: He plunged Germany into a deadly two front war. On the 18th of December 1940, while on the Obersalzberg, he issued directive „Barbarossa": to attack the USSR in order to open the living space in the East and render Germany secure against blockade.

# „I just keep a girl for me"

„Very intelligent men should take themselves a primitive and stupid woman."

Though Hitler carefully crafted the image of the elegant charmer, dog-lover and friend of children while on the Obersalzberg, he nonetheless delivered this insult in the presence of ladies (among them his companion Eva Braun) at one of his lengthy evening monologues.

On another occasion, during an evening monologue at the Berghof, he lectured: „The intellect of a woman makes absolutely no difference whatsoever. In comparison with educated, intellegent women, my mother was certainly an insignificant woman, but she has given the German people a great son."

Hitler considered marriage as unbearable for his „historic mission"; it forced him to squander his powers. „That is the worst thing about marriage: it creates legal rights! Thus it is much more proper to have a lover. The burden is removed. It is fortunate for me that I have not married. That would have become a disaster. A woman never understands that (in a marriage) the man does not find the time which the wife claims the right to have for herself."

Hitler detested „political women". The wife should dedicate herself to charitable tasks or the upbringing of youngsters. Indeed, a woman is superior to a man in matters of „practical understanding", such as when arranging an apartment. However, in politics, 99 percent of all subjects under consideration concern „matters of men, that women cannot judge".

Hitler ascertained that in the mountain highlands „the girls are completely wild about poachers". This provides evidence of the „natural instincts in a woman", who since the gray days of antiquity seeks a hero as a strong protector. However, if an excess of women exists (like in Germany), then the fight for men render even „the mildest woman a beast".

As an exception to this rule, Hitler cited the supposedly showpiece „Nordic master race" (tall, blond and blue-eyed Scandinavian men): „They are to such an extent so weak, that there even the most beautiful women move away if they get one of our men. So it was with Göring and his Carin" (Author's Note: his first wife, a Swede).

The man who thought in millennia wanted to privately spare himself such completely banal worries: „ I could never marry. If I would have children, what problems! In the end they would still try to make my son successor. Someone like me has no prospect of begetting a capable son. Look at Goethe's son, a completely useless person!" Besides (so he entrusted a war comrade in 1934), his entire energies belonged to the nation. In addition, as a married man he would have lost the vote of many women during elections. Thus he could not start a family. He would endure this like the pope. And in the jargon of a landowner (who keeps riding horses and breeding dogs), Hitler justified his extravagance: „So I just keep a girl for me in Munich." This girl had already in 1932 undertaken the first of two attempted suicides, because Hitler refused to marry. She entrusted her diary: „He only needs me for certain purposes." This girl was Eva Braun.

Born into the modest circumstances of a trade school teacher, this flagrantly vivacious, athletic, attractive girl attended a convent school. In 1929, the 40 year old Hitler became acquainted with the 17 year old Eva when she was employed by Hitler's personal photographer Heinrich Hofmann. And from 1932 onward they shared a life with one another according to Hitler's politically-conditioned, lower middle-class ideals: They never met publicly. During visits to Berchtesgaden, Eva initially roomed in a hotel, and only within the most narrow circle of confidants she appeared as a „secretary". She was always chauffeured

*In the company of privileged inner circle confidants Hitler made no secret of his relationship with Eva Braun. The wedding of Eva's sister Gretl with SS General Fegelein in 1944 provided an especially merry occasion. After the ceremony in Salzburg (Honor Witnesses Himmler & Bormann!) there was a boisterous party at the Berghof and Kehlsteinhaus. This photo stems from that event. First row, from right: Eva, Hitler, Gretl, Fegelein. In April 1945, Hitler had Fegelein shot because Fegelein wanted to flee from the fighting in Berlin.*

*Photo: Baumann*

„camouflaged" amongst two other Hitler secretaries in a closed Mercedes (hours before or after the official Hitler motorcade) on the Obersalzberg, so that nobody established a connection. And „covered" through two secretaries, Eva Braun could also participate in Hitlers walks on the Obersalzberg - though at the end of the column.

In 1935, Hitler rented a three room apartment in Munich for Eva. A year later he gave her a small villa. But because of the conspicuous police protection, which always attracted the curious, the Führer could only rarely visit his lover (and only at night). Therefore, in 1936, he made Eva the housekeeper in the renovated Berghof on the Obersalzberg.

Hitler's half sister Angela Raubal had functioned in this role since 1928. But uncle Adolf had cast an eye upon her lovely daughter Geli. According to the estimates of all witnesses, this was Hitler's great love. In the meantime this relationship displeased Geli's mother, but Hitler comforted her with the excuse that he must ensure „that Geli doesn't fall into the hands of any adventurer or swindler". Therefore in 1929 he brought the girl to Munich so that she could study there. However, Geli could not bear constantly being hidden before the public and being Hitler's neglected number two (behind politics). She committed suicide in 1931 at the age of 23 years.

This naturally clouded Hitler's relationship to his resolute half-sister, especially since now Eva also emerged on the Obersalzberg. Raubal privately scolded her as a „stupid cow", refused to shake her hand, and pointedly addressed her as „Miss". She also inventively ensured that none of the three bedrooms in the house was ever free; thus Eva had to reside in the ten minute distant Platterhof. Dresden architecture professor Hammitzsch solved these growing tensions when he married Angela Raubal in 1936.

Hitler retained his new housekeeper (formerly „secretary"; however, henceforth referred to as „boss lady" by the subservient souls wit-

hin the Berghof) only for certain presentable necessities - actually as long as she did not disturb his image.

A Führer with secret parlors for his concubine (at the Berghof, in Munich, and even in the Berlin Reichs Chancellory) - this is simply incredible, as occasionally recorded worries of party bigwigs and propagandists show.

Eva, on the contrary, who always addressed Hitler publicly as „my Führer", suffered from this hide-and-seek. And so once, at the Berghof, she confessed to the curious wife of Minister Esser: „Everything is so empty, if the Führer is not here. I would gladly dispense with the conveniences here, if I might be once again briefly near the Führer. Unfortunately, due to the division of his time and and his official importance, he takes absolutely no considerations for private things."

The majority of these private things transpired in the lonely monotony on the Obersalzberg - amidst the „surrogate family" of secretaries, adjutants, household staff and motor pool personnel. Hitler's very presence intensified this monotony of a rigid daily routine, a notoriously frugal dietary regimen, the viewing of banal films and endless monologues. These had the habit of stretching the evening fireplace chats well into the following morning, and regularly forced the fearful listeners to fight the fatigue of heavy eyelids.

Father Braun considered this illegitimate relationship of his daughter as dishonorable. Thus in the Autumn of 1935 he took it to heart and asked the „Right Honorable Mr. Chancellor" (in writing) if Eva could return „to the family." Brown asked the photographer Hofmann to forward this letter; however, Hofmann submitted the correspondence to Eva (who tore it up). Mother Braun also wrote their „son-in-law"; indeed, without any detours. She never received an answer.

In the Berlin Reich Chancellory Eva spent her brief stays behind drawn curtains in a secluded suite. And in the Berghof she always had to amuse herself in an elegant, spacious

*Eva Braun, Hitler's unhappy companion, with her dogs at the Berghof. „He only needs me for certain purposes", confided Eva in her diary. Hitler rigorously kept her from public view. Eva suffered under such loneliness that she undertook two suicide attempts.*                    Photo: Baumann

room (adjacent to Hitler's quarters) with records, films or her dogs, if Hitler conferred or banqueted with prominents.

Several of the „chosen" ladies of the prominent Nazis who had settled on the Obersalzberg flagrantly insulted her. They cut her down or treated her with aloofness. For instance, in the summer of 1937, Mrs. Göring once „forgot" to invite Eva to one of the occasional parties for the Obersalzberg ladies. Whereupon Hitler summoned Göring for a harangue: „Fräulein Braun is, of course, with her 25 years still too young and inexperienced to be the First Lady of the Third Reich. She is, however, the only woman in my life. I will marry her if I return to Linz one day for retirement. I wish that this is respected!"

This became especially apparent with Hitler's omnipotent Secretary Bormann (who was himself infamous as the biggest „Reichs skirt chaser"). This awkward and malicious man made Eva feel that she was not attainable. But after Hitler's upbraiding of Göring, Bormann read every wish of her eyes, because he now estimated her as an influential ally against „the Fat One."

Yet another especially cultivated Obersalzberg resident, Hitler's architect Albert Speer, very soon felt sympathy for the unhappy Eva, who was so hung-up on Hitler. He described her as politically disinterested, „with a healthy outlook toward the realities of everyday life", and as simply clothed. Among other things, she wore „strikingly cheap jewelry of insulting modesty" - holiday presents from Hitler. A noteworthy exception: A tourmaline ring along with matching ear rings and a bracelet, which she received for her 21st birthday on 6 February 1933.

This present was well overdue. After all, Hitler had been appointed seven days previously - on 30 January - as Reichs Chancellor. And three days earlier - on 3 February - he had presented his concept to the military leadership: The priority of rearmament, extermination of the „cancerous ulcer" democracy, conquest,

and the „indiscriminate Germanization" of new living space in the East. That was well worth a generous present for Eva.

Speer once arranged a winter vacation for the enthusiastic skier Eva from Hitler (who strictly forbid her dancing, smoking and sunbathing in swim costume). For a week she participated in winter sports with the Speers in Zürs, and danced in the evening with unsuspecting officers. This was an extremely rare pleasure if one considers Hitlers dislike of dancing - be it to „Nigger music" (jazz) or waltzes.

For instance, in 1928 friends urged the 39 year old non-dancer Hitler to sharpen his social skills with a dance course, especially since even George Washington, Napoleon and Frederick the Great were excellent dancers. Hitler considered dancing as unsuitable for a statesman. Besides, „walzes were much too feminine for a man". The „Walz mania" absolutely accelerated the demise of the Habsburg Empire.

Apparently the social skills which his well-heeled „motherly friends" of the Twenties in their Munich drawing-rooms had provided him sufficed for Hitler: A well-versed hand kiss introduction (with implied „Austrian charm") as well as decent clothes belonged to good social skills.

These mature ladies were fond of this true German, ambitious, eloquent and always obliging young politician, and thus provided contacts in the best circles of the Munich society. Among the influential contacts made were the wives of piano manufacturer Bechstein and the publisher Bruckmann.

Thus it disturbed Hitler by no means to maintain distant friendships with self-confident and professionally successful ladies that were correspondingly and completely out of character with his image of women such as with Winifred Wagner, the Mistress of Bayreuth, or director Leni Riefenstahl. These women enabled him, the social outsider, to gain entrance to the caste of scorned „plutocrats." However,

*Hitler banished Eva Braun to the role of „housekeeper" on the Obersalzberg - and ordered her to her room if unknowing prominent visitors came around. This vivacious, uncomplicated young woman spent her time with animals, records, films and a yearning for the Führer. He finally rewarded her faithfulness with marriage shortly before their dual suicide on 30 April 1945 in the „Führer Bunker" under the remnants of the Berlin Reichs Chancellory.* Photo: Baumann

*Hitler's relationship with Eva Braun was nearly a state secret. Naturally rumors circulated around the World about this relationship. Indeed, those in Germany who passed on such rumors or even jokes risked concentration camp imprisonment. Eva Braun's life within the sterile, monotonous Obersalzberg surrogate family of secretaries, adjutants and housekeeping personnel was tabu.* Photo: Baumann

as helpers in the ascension to power they were irreplaceable to Hitler. From such women he even accepted something which he otherwise never bore: Criticism.

Famous among insiders were the tongue-lashings that Mrs. Bechstein dispensed even before witnesses upon Chancellor Hitler because of political questions: The rhetorical question, whether he was crazy, followed by a flood of insults. Meanwhile, Hitler stood there during these dressing-downs like a wet poodle.

On the Obersalzberg, Hitler would certainly not allow that to happen.

# Hitler - the Mass Murderer

Henriette von Schirach, daughter of Hitler's personal photographer Heinrich Hofmann and wife of the Gauleiter (NSDAP district chief) of Vienna, triggered an unprecedented scandal at the Berghof on Good Friday of 1943.

Just returned from the Netherlands, she indignantly described at Hitler's evening fireplace chat how Jewesses were hustled by the Gestapo and SS through the streets of Amsterdam en route to deportation. She had nothing against „deportation" of the Jews to the East, but with such brutal turmoil?

Embarrassed silence. For a while Hitler bored through Frau Schirach with a stare, and then suddenly he screamed at her: „You are sentimental! What have you to worry about the Jewish women! This is all sentimentality!" Hitler raged further. Meanwhile, Frau Schirach hurried to her room. There she was cornered by an adjutant: „Why have you done that? You have made him so angry. Depart at once. Immediately!"

Shortly before, Henriette's husband, the enthusiastic Germanic poet and „Reichs Youth Leader" Baldur von Schirach, had already forfeited his last goodwill with Hitler because of an exhibition, „Young Art in the Third Reich" in Vienna. There hung pictures which Hitler considered as „degenerated" according to his understanding of art. Hitler summoned Schirach to the Obersalzberg, shoved a photographic report about this exhibition in front of his nose and hissed: „A green-colored dog! With this you mobilize all the culture Bolshevists against me. This is education for the opposition!" The exhibition was immediately closed.

*Due to the impression of increasing Allied bombing raids, the military security for Obersalzberg began in 1943 with the construction of 5 km of tunnels and 4,000 square meters of luxurious „living rooms" inside the mountain. In addition, 10 air defense batteries with 54 guns were placed around the Obersalzberg. Up to 2,000 SS soldiers served duty at these facilities.* Photo: Baumann

Degenerative, „Jew-plagued", Bolshevistic - such were the inflammatory leitmotifs of the racist Hitler. But neither he personally nor Himmler, Goebbels or Bormann corresponded to his ideal of the „Nordic master race": Tall, blond, blue-eyed.

During his years of dawdling in Vienna, Hitler had devoured large quantities of mystical, racist nonsense about Aryans, Jews and Slavs. He was infuriated about the „lecherous look" with which shabby „caftan Jews" pursue blond girls.

This ultimately formed Hitler's racist antisemitism: Jews are the originators of social democracy and communism; Jews controlled the stock exchanges, labor movements and culture; Jews held the farmers in economic exploitation; Jews are vermin and parasites in every healthy people - therefore they need to be eradicated.

In 1922, during an outburst of hatred, the 33 year old Hitler explained to his war comrade Josef Hell: „ If I ever come to power, then the destruction of the Jews will be my first and foremost task. For example, as soon as I have the power, I'll set up gallows beside the Marienplatz in Munich. Then the Jews will be hanged, and they will stay there so long until they stink. Then the next ones will have their turn, until the last Jew in Munich is obliterated. This will proceed in exactly this manner, until Germany is purified of the last Jew." From half-educated German nationalists in Vienna, Hitler also culled more prejudices about the „eastern subhumans", the Slavs.

Because of the impression of Germany's defeat in 1918, the ensuing democratic revolution and the „Dictate of Versailles", these ideas further proliferated into a warlike plan of conquest: The German people need a blockade-secure living space in the East.

Hitler's dictatorship depended upon Gestapo terror, propaganda and job creation through rearmament. Thereby the Christian and the economic antisemitism in the population proved very useful to Hitler. Both helped him to incite people from one antisemitic „event" to the next, and thus he diverted them from multiple problems.

Among the „events" to transpire: The boycott of Jewish businesses because a London tabloid had printed an absurd, insignificant „Declaration of War by the World Jewry" against Germany; the Nürnberg „Race Laws", which took away the basic rights of Jews and separated the „foreign-blooded citizens from the naturally born citizens"; the expulsion of Jews from the ranks of civil service, profession and art; the officially mandated surnames „Sarah" and „Israel" for Jews, along with a „J" in the passport and ultimately the yellow star of David on clothing. All the while, the brown hordes roared „Germany awaken - death to Judah".

In 1938, a young Jew delivered the (for the time being) welcomed occasion for the most depraved of antisemitic excesses. He had assinated a German diplomat in Paris as revenge for the maltreatment of his parents during their expulsion to Poland. Thereupon the Nazis „spontaneously" instigated the „Reichs Crystal Night". In this orgy of violence and fire 191 synagogues and 171 apartment houses were set ablaze, 7,500 businesses were plundered, 91 Jews were murdered and 26,000 Jews were taken into „protective custody".

The infamous revenge of the Nazis had been very effective: As a „redemption" of this pogrom, the German Jews were collectively condemned to pay compensation to the insurance companies and also to remit an „Atonement Payment" of 3.15 billion euro (monetary value 2007). The decree of Jewish exclusion from German business was yet another harsh consequence. This was called „Aryanization" and was blatant expropriation of businesses.

Most German Jews did not comprehend (or for that matter had no more money) that immediate emigration was their last chance.

In his pompously programmatic book „Mein Kampf" (1925), Hitler qualified Jews as „parasites in the body of other People, which poison the blood of others". It is also written: „There cannot be two chosen people. We are the people of God. Two worlds face one another! God's people and Satan's people, the Aryan and the Jew." And as early as 1933 Hitler threatened: „If I send the cream of the Germans into the steel storm of the coming war, should I not then have the right to eliminate millions of an inferior, increasing-like-vermin race?"

On the eve of World War II (30 January 1939), however, the planner of the largest war of aggression in the 20th Century further taunted (in inimitable infamy) his „racially and biologically worthless" whipping boys: „If it should be once again possible for international Jewry to throw people into a World War, then the result will not be a victory for Jewry, but the destruction of the Jewish race in Europe."

Several indications point to the fact that Hitler discussed the approach to the „final solution of the Jewish question" amidst the innermost circle of Nazi conspirators. He apparently placed the guidelines for industrially organized mass murder before Göring, Himmler and Heydrich on the Obersalzberg in 1941. This subsequently resulted in the concrete plan for industrially organized mass murder: „evacuation" of Jews in East European „special areas". Strictly speaking, Hitler fought against Britons and Frenchmen on the racially ideological „wrong" front. The „proper" thrust aimed at „Living Space in the East". The infamous Wannsee Conference of 20 January 1942 would ultimately determine „the implementation of the final solution of the Jewish Question" - the „biological substance" of the Jews, who numbered 9.2 million in Poland, Hungary, Rumania and in the Soviet Union.

This conference decided on a method which Hitler's Propaganda Minister Goebbels had called „destruction through work" - exploitation of Jewish energy for the German war industry. Indeed, the „most resistant portion" of the Jews who endured this „natural selection"

were to be treated separately, so that „no avengers for our sons and grandsons become adults". Therefore Goebbels declared the Jews as „unconditionally exterminable".

For its part, the officer corps also yielded itself, as Field Marshal General Reichenau proved with his infamous order of 10 October 1941: The war in the East is an „annihilation struggle against the Jewish-Bolshevist system". That made the soldiers „porters of an inexorable national idea and the avengers for all bestialities" against German culture. Consequently the soldier must have a full understanding for the „necessity of the hard, but just atonement against the Jewish sub-race". Hitler praised this order as „excellent", whereupon it was extended to all army forces in the East.

Meanwhile, the eradication of the Jews had provided unexpected problems for the SS „task forces" after the attack on Poland. These „special units" pursued „the most total possible abolition of Jewry". For example, on 31 January 1942 they bragged about „execution of up to now 229,052 Jews" in the Baltic states alone. Another report indeed criticized: „Nothing would be objectionable about the very numerous executions of Jews, if one would not simply leave the executed where they lay." Ultimately, one can neither poison nor shoot millions of Jews.

Therefore Hitler contrived other „actions", which merely began on 1 September 1939 with the defeaning noise of the attack on Poland. On this day Hitler ordered the murder of „useless eaters", and 115,000 handicapped people fell victim to „euthanasia" - predominantly through exhaust fumes which were pumped into camouflaged gas chambers. In September 1939 the planned extermination of roughly 500,000 gipsys also began.

This was the career leap of Hitler the military aggressor to Hitler the mass murderer.

On the 8th of December 1941, the industrially organized mass murder of the Jews began at the Polish extermination camp in Chelm-

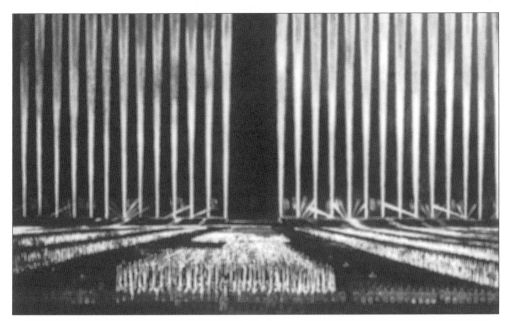

*The conventions of the Nazy Party in Nürnberg were among the well-honed self portrayals of the Nazi regime. Marching formations and columns of searchlight beams strengthened the self-confidence of po-wer and greatness. Hitler's evening appearance and speech at the Nürnberg Party Convention gained effectiveness through this scene.*                                                    *Photo: State Archives*

*In April 1943 Hitler once said that it would be dreadful if the Berghof would become a museum after his death. The Allies dispersed this worry with the bombing raid of 25 April 1945. Only a smoke blacke-ned ruin remained of the Berghof. This was later demolished.*                          *Photo: Baumann*

no - according to the official jargon for people „not able to work". And directly thereafter the program was conducted according to the standards of the Wannsee Conference: Summary of all Jews within Hitler's sphere of influence in the transient ghettos; if unable to work, „selection" for immediate gassing (initially with carbon monoxide, later with the vastly more effective Zyklon B); total exploitation of work-capable Jews for the war industry; ultimately gassing and cremation in the extermination camps at Chelmno, Belzec, Sobibor, Majdanek, Treblinka and Auschwitz -Birkenau.

On 27 March 1942, Goebbels confided to his diary: „A somewhat barbaric process is applied here, and not much remains from the Jews themselves. Even here the Führer is the undisputed champion of a radical solution."

The record of a conference with Hitler in August 1942 also reveals this militant role regarding „final solution of the Jewish question".

Thereby the accountant of the „final solution" in Poland, the SS Commander and former Viennese Gauleiter Odilo Globocnik, explained: „Gentlemen, if another generation should come after us which is so weak and so cowardly that they do not understand our great task (Author's Note: annihilation of the Jews), then all of National Socialism has been for nothing. I am on the contrary of the opinion that one should set bronze plaques in the mass graves of Jews with the inscription that we have had the courage to complete this great and necessary achievement."

Hitler's commentary: „Good Globocnik, that is indeed also my view!"

This blindly raging racial hatred seduced Hitler to such incredible nonsense that he obviated nuclear physics as „Jewish physics", and therefore also rejected the development of the atomic bomb as militarily useless (at any rate the time and means were insufficient).

And thus the man who stroked children on the Obersalzberg also had millions of Jews on his conscience: At least 3 million gassed and at least 2 million victims of the „task forces", the „extermination through work" and the „ghetto-cleansing".

And that man, who himself attended to charmingly elegant ladies in the Berghof, and as circumspect man of the house even examined the placesettings before festive meals, lectured to his table companions: „We will only attain health if we eradicate the Jews." Still on 2 April 1945 he dictated to his Secretary Bormann: „One will be eternally grateful that I have extinguished the Jews in Europe."

However, the man who played with dogs and caressed fawns on the Obersalzberg remained an unrestrained Hater until his suicide on 30 April 1945 in the Führer Bunker under the ruins of the Berlin Reichs Chancellory. His will of the previous day ends with this deranged, infernal sentence: „Above all I obligate the leadership of the nation and its adherents to the painstaking observance of the racial laws and to the merciless resistance against the most world-poisonous of all people, - international Jewry."

# Hitler - the War Criminal

21 August 1939, supper in the Berghof. An orderly gave Hitler a piece of paper. Hitler glanced through it, stared for a moment, turned red, and suddenly hammered his fists on the table. „Now I have them, now I have them", he screamed in a wavering voice. Hitler immediatedly calmed himself down, silently finished the meal and finally proclaimed: „We will sign a non-aggression treaty with Russia. Here, read Stalin's telegram."

The path was cleared to the sensation of 24 August - the pact between ice and fire. Rightwing totalitarian Hitler and left-wing totalitarian Stalin had thus arranged the division of

*Leisure time on the Obersalzberg. Reichs Marshal Göring, responsible among other things for the war economy and the air force, gladly posed as a sportsman and even undertook a rock climbing tour on Little Watzmann Mountain while fastened to the ropes of mountain guides. Hitler participated in absolutely no sport, although he urgently recommended this to Germans - above all the Youth: „Quick as a greyhound, tough as leather, hard as Krupp steel." Hitler amused himself on the Obersalzberg with a daily walk to the tea house on the Mooslahnerkopf. In this photo, notice the dagger that Göring (in civil attire) gladly wore on his belt as an emblem of his title as „Reichs Master Hunter".* Photo: Baumann

*Hitler, the party chief. Upon this dictatorial role the official party handbook of 1936 formulated „the precepts of National Socialists: The Führer is always right! The program should be dogma; it demands utmost devotion to the Movement! Proper is what serves the Movement and therewith Germany! The Führer Corps is responsible for the total penetration of the German people in the National Socialist spirit. The Führer's will is the foremost law of the Party."*
Photo: State Archives

Poland and the delimitation of the Interest Zones in Eastern Europe. Of course this ensured Hitler's deadline for the 1 September attack on Poland, but contradicted his prophecy from „Mein Kampf": Any German-Russian alliance inevitably leads to a war „that means the end of Germany". What weight carried now the swastika armbands being thrown by hundreds of party members over the fence of party headquarters in Munich as a protest against the treacherous pact with the „Jewish-Bolshevist tyranny"?

Hitler had his triumph, which he had argued (on the morning after Stalin's telegram) before the gathered military commanders on the Obersalzberg: „Now Poland is in the position in which I wanted to have them. We do not need to fear a blockade (by the Western powers). The East will deliver us grain, cattle, coal, lead, zinc. I will provide the propagandist occasion for the declaration of war, irregardless whether it is plausible or not. The victor will not be asked afterwards, whether he said the truth or not. Starting a war is not a question of righteouness, but of victory."

On that morning Hitler received a free path to the peak of his career. And he surprised the world with a „lightning war" concept: attacks prepared with heavy blows of a powerful air force and propelled by huge, highly mobile tank divisions.

On the 1st of September Hitler attacked Poland, and on the 27th Warsaw capitulated. Although treaties with Poland immediatedly pulled England and France into the war, both states still did not use the chance to attack the weak German West Front. In April 1940 Hitler took Denmark and Norway in an attempt to secure the supply of Swedish ore - and thereby anticipated the British by only a few days. On the 10th of May, Hitler ended the „Sitzkrieg" in the West and subjugated the neutral states Holland and Belgium as well as France within 42 days. Meanwhile, even Göring's first great defeat at Dunkirk in June 1940 changed nothing. The Reichs Marshal wanted to take care of the 338,000 soldiers of the British Expeditionary Army (who were trapped along the coast) with his air force, and obtained from Hitler an order for the pursuing tank divisions to stop before Dunkirk. However, for several days Dunkirk lay obscured under the dense smoke of oil tanks burning in the harbor. Therefore Göring's „Luftwaffe" was not able to see the British army escape across the English Channel.

Now however, as the armed forces celebrated Hitler as the greatest commander of all time, misfortune unveiled itself: Hitler had „proven" his military infallibility, and henceforth no longer listened to the advice of his generals.

What an ascent for a man who had begun his career with social descent. But the huge parade in Berlin after the victory over France was Hitler's last triumph. The stubborness of a man who was himself considered one of the most knowledgeable and versatile militarily technical specialists of his time only hardened. Nevertheless he remained militarily the dilettante, who did not comprehend the sense of systematic technical knowledge and instead confused a laymans resolve with the „intuition" of a mastermind. Hitler remained the half-educated, who certainly didn't know everything, but certainly knew everything better - incapable of self-criticism, proven in no profession.

„Yes, here my thoughts ripen." So did Hitler once praise the advantage of his historic stage on the Obersalzberg. He added that here he found the internal quiet and assurance for his surprising decisions. And certainly here surprising decisions also shoved him off balance.

Consequently, on 11 May 1941, around noon, an adjutant of the Führer's deputy Rudolf Hess burst into Hitler's daily meeting with an urgent letter. Hitler scanned the correspondence and flew into a raging fit as he read that Hess had wanted to fly the previous evening to Scotland in order to undertake peace negotiations with England: „Hopefully he will crash into the sea!" However, the undesirable dove of peace had long since landed by parachute at his goal (and then into internment). Hess had under technical pretenses provided his ME-110 with supplementary fuel tanks for the lengthy flight route.

The raging Hitler seized Hess' written suggestion and declared him crazy (in the event that this peace mission displeased the British). Propaganda Chief Goebbels promptly circulated the explanation that Hess suffered the initial symptoms of derangement and depression.

*The self portrayal of statesman Hitler amidst the powerful scenery of the Obersee. A psychologically revealing detail: Hitler holds a horse riding whip in his hand.*

Photo: State Archives

This portrayal was plausible, because as Hitler's Secretary in Munich (for 945 euro per month, monetary value 2007), and later as Hitler's Party Deputy, Hess had offered ample occasion for such evaluations.

He was considered not only as Hitler's „most devoted subordinate" and as a mad fighter pilot who „even flies through barn doors". One considered him at least distressingly eccentric, because he surrounded himself with soothsayers, non-medical practitioners, nature apostles, fortune tellers, astrologers and occultists. Therefore the angry Hitler immediately arrested such people from Hess' circle of friends and also generally forbid such practices. On the next day (13 May 1941), Hitler summoned all Gauleiters and party ministers to the Obersalzberg. He declared that this breach of trust by Hess represented one of the blackest days of his career - at a time when „our divisions (in the East) are on the alert and at any hour could receive the order to commence their most difficult military deployment ever". The brown elite understood: „Operation Barbarossa" - the attack on the USSR - was impending. However, Hitler trembled: Would Hess betray to the British the unusually cleverly camouflaged deployment in the East (3.2 million men; 600,000 motor vehicles; 3,580 tanks; 2,740 airplanes and 7,184 guns)? No, Hess betrayed nothing.

On 13 May 1941, a „military court order" was delivered to army forces: Civilians in the East are not subject to military court jurisdiction; excesses of soldiers against civilians are not necessarily to be punished. The SS („on the authority of the Führer") now exercised „special tasks" that result from „the ultimate struggle of two opposing political systems". The infamous „Provisional Commissar Order" less vaguely defined these „special tasks" : Liquidation of political commissars, Jews and Orthodox clergy.

Both orders set in concrete what Hitler had proposed (as a leitmotif for the conquest of new living space) to the military leadership on 30 March 1941: „This is a war of extermination. We do not wage war to preserve the enemy."

The narrow-minded racist Hitler thus dismissed the instinctive politician Hitler, and lost the immensely strategic chance to gain advantages from the brutal minority politics of Lenin and Stalin. Ukrainians, Belorussians and other Soviet peoples had initially celebrated the German army as liberators - until the „task forces" and SS taught them with uninhibited brutality what SS chief Himmler had determined in a May 1940 memorandum. According to Himmler, the „leaderless worker folk" in the East has to master only three things in the future: „Count to 500, write their name, know the 10 Commandments, and be obedient, honest, diligent and good to the Germans." This insanity allowed Stalin to unite the people of the USSR for its „Great Patriotic War", and thus even to receive the blessings of the heretofore brutally persecuted Orthodox church.

On 22 June 1941 Hitler invaded the Soviet Union in „Blitzkrieg" strategy and drove the Red Army from one destructive encirelement battle to the next; and this transpired in such a tempo that troop commanders groaned: „Before us no enemy, behind us no supply." Five months later the „Blitzkrieg" and Hitler's strategic Latin terminated in the minefields and blizzards before Moscow.

Neo-brown fablers gladly blame Mussolini for this failure (the attack on the USSR had begun around six weeks too late, thereby Moscow could no longer be conquered). This argumentation conceals the fact that not the conquest of Moscow, but the endless expanse and inexhaustible reserves of Russia were the decisive factors.

Indeed, in the Spring of 1941 Hitler actually had to help his flashy Italian alliance partner out of two humiliating predicaments: In February 1941, the legendary „Africa Corps" (under the leadership of „Desert Fox" General Erwin Rommel) jumped into North Africa, because the Italians (during an attempted advance out of their Libyan colony toward Egypt) were threatened with imminent defeat by the British.

Two months later Hitler occupied Yugoslavia and Greece to create order in the Balkans. Tiny Greece had already chased the Italians out of a third of Albania, a country which Mussolini, in an attack of megalomania, had occupied in 1939 and had expanded as the basis for an invasion of Greece.

That cost Hitler substantial time, manpower and material. At any rate, Mussolini's misadventures in North Africa and in the Balkans changed nothing in the turn of events during the disaster which Hitler accelerated on 11 December 1941 with his declaration of war against the USA.

Three days earlier the Japanese had attacked Pearl Harbor.

Hitler (in a display of fanatical arrogance) immediatedly leaped to the aid of his Japanese alliance partners against „Nigger-plagued" USA - an industrial power which lay beyond Germany's range and within two years surpassed twofold the entire combined war production capability of Germany, Italy and Japan.

In March 1942, the Allies commenced the air war against German cities. The war-deciding „paralyzation" of the German home front began in May 1944 within a few days, as Hitler once again was recovering on the Obersalzberg from his endeavors:

Massive attacks on hydrocarbon plants (= production of gasoline from coal) reduced the German daily fuel production from 7,000 to 120 metric tons.

Therewith the hope of a supposedly war-deciding „wonder weapon" disappeared: The few models from the first series of the jet fighter did not leave the ground. And the rockets proved themselves as a premature failure: These „V - weapons" were intended as revenge for the allied bombing raids, and had a range of up to 350 km; however, they transported much fewer explosives than bombers. They were also inaccurate and were frequently shot down because they flew slower than the fighter planes of the Allies.

On 3 November 1942, the „Africa Corps" suffered a decisive defeat (for the Africa war) at El Alamein. Four days later the Americans and British landed in Morocco and Algeria. On the 13th of May 1943, over 260,000 German and Italian soldiers capitulated in Tunis. At Casablanca in January 1943, the Allies committed themselves to the unconditional capitulation of Germany, Italy and Japan, which does not mean „the annihilation of the population" of these countries, but of imperialistic world politics.

In February 1943, Hitler suffered a war-deciding defeat (in the East) through the disaster of the 280,000 man army encircled in Stalingrad.

18 days afterwards, in the Berlin Sport Palace, Goebbels harvested the frenetic consent of the brown elite when posing the rhetorical question: „ Do you want total war? Do you want it, if necessary, totally and more radically than we can even imagine today?"

Five months later the allies landed on Sicily. On the 10th of September 1943, they conquered Rome.

In May 1943, Hitler - once again vacationing at the Berghof - broke off the „Battle of the Atlantic", the systematic attacks on American supply routes to Europe, because of devastating submarine losses. Out of 39,000 sailors in German submarines, only 6,000 survived the war.

# Hitler - the National Traitor

A new day dawned upon the Salzburg Alps on 6 June 1944. As usual, on the previous evening Hitler had held long monologues at the Berghof and watched a film before he went to bed at two o'clock in the morning. At around 3 o'clock, news of the invasion of Normandy by substantial paratroop units alarmed the Obersalzberg. Three hours later the first report about the beginning of the invasion followed. However, nobody dared to wake Hitler, because this was surely the expected „decoy attack", a falsified attack plan which the British had allegedly allowed the German command to intercept.

As usual, Hitler got up around 10 o'clock to breakfast - and began to rage after he finally looked through the first messages. Invasion or not? Was this an Allied feint to divert German forces from the „main attack" in the Strait of Calais, as Hitler was certain? At any rate, according to Hitler's view: „If the invasion is not beaten back, the war is lost for us."

A half day later Hitler even presented himself in the Platterhof, before hundreds of representatives of the armaments industry, in a mood of gallows humor: „If this war becomes a lost cause, gentlemen, then it only remains that each individual consider his private shift from this World to the other World beyond: whether he wants to do that personally, or whether he wants to hang himself, or whether he wants to be given a shot in the neck."

In the historic review this mockery functions

*The bombing raid of 25 April 1945 transformed the Obersalzberg into a heap of ruins, which the U.S. Army Air Corps later documented in photographic detail (thus the U.S. aircraft in the middle of the photo). At right in the photo one recognizes the ruin of „Hotel Türken"; above the kindergarten, SS barracks and large garage for duty vehicles. From the right, the destroyed road comes into view and curves towards the destroyed greenhouse facility, whose concrete foundation walls and expanse serve today as a parking lot. At lower left in the photo is the ruin of Bormann's house.* Photo: State Archives

*Until the large scale renovation of 1935/36, the original „Haus Wachenfeld" was sufficient for „People's Chancellor Hitler", although already enlarged with terrace, winter garden and garages. The wide driveway to the parking lot already lay within the enfenced and stringently guarded „Führer Area", before which the curious thronged to catch a glimpse of the Führer. This photo was taken from the viewpoint of Gasthof „Türken". It is understandable that this house was requisitioned by Hitler's guard detachment, and only after the war - as a ruin - given back to the owners.* Photo: Baumann

macabrely, because the mass murderer and war criminal Hitler had long since overstepped the threshold to high treason against Germany: He refused the unavoidable capitulation and unscrupulously sacrificed millions of Germans to extend his own life.

Shortly before the attack on Poland, Hitler had given this leitmotif: „As long as I live, nothing will be spoken of capitulation."

After the attack on Poland, Hitler appeared in military uniform before the parliament: „Once again I wear that coat which is for me is most sacred and cherished. I will only remove it after victory - or I will never experience such an end."

Hitler had repeatedly placed in prospect what he pondered in the event of failure: „Then I'll finish it in five minutes with a pistol."

In the self-splendor of a boundless dictator, Hitler had already in 1924 retorted an internal party competitor: „I never err, all of my words are historic."

Hitler's scorn of the conservatives who previously had thoroughly welcomed him into a coalition as a political „horseman's groom" in 1934 is also revealing: „They are all mistaken. They underestimate me, because I come from below, because I have no education, because I do not know how to behave in a manner that they - in their sparrow brains - consider proper. I do not need them to confirm my historic greatness."

At the Berghof in 1936, Hitler boasted before Munich's Cardinal Faulhaber (of all people!) in his characteristic „either-or" manner: „There are two possibilities for me: To succeed with my plans or to fail. If I succeed, then I'll become of one the Greats of history. If I fail, I will be condemned, detested and damned."

In November 1939, Hitler addressed the gathered generals: „As the last factor, I must in all modesty name my own persona: irreplaceable. The fate of the Reich depends solely on me."

Three months previously, he had emphasized to a representative of the League of Nations (precursor of the postwar UNO): „I will relentlessly fight to the end."

An inconceivably cynical remark during Christmas 1941 confirms that Hitler comprehended quite well what happened in the „snowy desert" before Moscow and what he thought of the Germans: „If the German people are no longer strong enough and prepared to sacrifice their own blood for their existence, then it should happen that they are destroyed by another stronger force. Then I will shed no tears for the German people."

Naturally the Germans shed their blood by no means for their existence. They had to sacrifice it for Hitler's obligatory megalomania.

Thus Hitler logically issued the „Nero Order" (sabotaged by Armaments Minister Speer) to the armed forces and all Gauleiters on 19 March 1945. All facilities for traffic, supplies and industry, as well as all material assets in the remaining German-controlled territory were to be destroyed, because: „ The people have proven themselves as the weaker, and the future belongs exclusively to the stronger East Folk. What remains after this struggle are merely the inferior, because the best have fallen."

In comparison, although it was habitually branded by the brown „Old Aryans", the plan of US

*After the war the Berghof ruins became a popular excursion destination. The masonry down to the concrete foundation was demolished to prevent this place from degenerating into a political pilgrimage site. Today the uphill terrain alongside the road from Berchtesgaden is forested.* Photo: Baumann

*After the bombing raid of 25 April 1945, only a mass of rubble remained of Hitler's Berghof. The U.S. Army Air Corps photographically documented the scene (thus the U.S. aircraft in the middle of the photo). On the left above the Berghof, one sees the kindergarten and to the right rear the SS barracks. This area today is fully reforested. The remnants of the Berghof and SS barracks foundations are still recognizable beneath the overgrowth of shrubbery.*      Photo: State Archives

Secretary of Commerce Morgenthau seemed simply paradise-like: A defeated Germany must be transformed into an agrarian country so that it can never instigate a war again. President Roosevelt rejected that idea.

Hitler intensified the high treason against the German people with the infamous remark that labelled survivors as „inferior" - after he had squandered the „best" in the „storms of steel" during his unscrupulous war of aggression.

Thus the Berghof as a means of Hitler's political self-staging shifts once again into the picture: Up until the victory over France it was embossed with the image of a child and animal loving, affable vacationer and a civilian-clothed private individual. Increasingly, Hitler also posed as a statesmanlike host for publicity-effective prominents.

After the reconstruction of the Berghof, Hitler received former British Premier Lloyd George in 1936, while in the year thereafter he hosted the Duke of Windsor (who had relinquished the British crown because of his marriage to a divorced American).

In February 1938, Hitler summoned the Austrian Federal Chancellor Kurt Schuschnigg to the Obersalzberg in order to set the trap (by demanding unfulfillable stipulations) for Austria's „annexation" a month later.

Because of the „Sudeten crisis", Hitler coerced the aging British Premier Neville Chamberlain into a journey to the Obersalzberg in September 1938.

Altogether, from the Summer of 1936 up until 14 July 1944 -Hitler's final departure from the Obersalzberg - 39 guests in the rank of official state visitors or ambassadors were registered at the Berghof. Of this total, 13 visits were in times of peace. 23 guests were alliance partners or satellites like Croatia, Slovakia, Rumania and Bulgaria. Italian Foreign Minister Ciano came six times, Mussolini twice, and Japan's Ambassador Oshima three times. On the other hand, the list of visitors also illustrates Hitler's international isolation. This occurred as a result of the attack on the Soviet Union in June 1941, and also coincides with Hitler's increasing loneliness.

After the first failures he increasingly avoided the public. He refused to leave his spirit world or to visit bombed-out cities in order to cheer up the people there. Instead, he wallowed in the imaginary world of future „castles in the air" architecture for Berlin and Linz.

The great defeats during the turn of the year 1942/43 exposed Hitler's weakness of leadership: He was missing the successes which would have enabled him to demagogically dupe the masses. He blamed (in unprecedented infamy) the „German People" for this lack of success.

In 1945, the „All or Nothing" gambler Hitler stood before the Nothing. Then he grasped a pistol and escaped responsibility. Within 12 years he had caused the contrary to everything which he had promised and striven for: Germany was destroyed.

*„Hail Victory, to our People's Chancellor." So greeted the triumph-arch above the gate before Haus Wachenfeld the landlord in the Spring of 1933. A representative of the SA (left) and SS were still sufficient as guards along the narrow, steep driveway. And yet the construction shed already signalled great changes befitting the needs of the Chancellor and party chief. A winter garden, large terrace, spacious garage and large parking lot as well as a wider, graded driveway were later built. Twelve years later this site - and Hitler's imperialistic „Third Reich" - was a pile of ruins.*          Photo: Baumann

Seven million Germans died for nothing. 12 million Germans were expelled by the East European victims of the aggressor Hitler. 33 million people in other European countries were killed. Germany and Europe remained a half century divided, while astronomical sums were squandered for armament. Europe was power-politically downgraded, while the USSR and the USA besieged the world with cold war caused by Moscow.

Even today the world retains a multitude of memorials, terms of horror, or documentations of cruelty as a legacy to Hitler's crime scenes. For instance: the concentration camps at Dachau, Buchenwald or Mauthausen; the extermination camps like Auschwitz; sites of ingeniously agonizing executions of regime opponents like Berlin-Plötzensee.

The remnants of Hitler's crime scenes such as „Wolf's Lair" at Rastenburg in Masuria and the Obersalzberg differ from the sites of terror and murder orgies. They were the command and control centers of the most evil mastermind in history, who never soiled his well-groomed fingers with blood.

Nothing remains of the „Wolf's Lair" but cyclopean heaps of scattered concrete chunks, on which moss and lichen proliferate: Oppressing gloom in an endless forest.

The Obersalzberg, on the contrary, is a recivilized holiday paradise, far removed from Hitler's crimes. The grandiose surrounding countryside seduces the thoughts to a Potemkin-like facade, before which an elegant civilian kissed the hands of ladies, caressed children, and stroked both dogs and fawns. Nobody was tortured, choked, stabbed, shot dead or gassed.

The decisive difference between both these stages of the most wicked all masterminds certainly lies therein: In the „Wolf's Lair", one remembers today the men and women of that better Germany, who on 20 July 1944 dared the plot against Hitler, and atoned for their failure with their life. However among the visitors in the ruins of the Obersalzberg you find still „fans" of Germany's national traitor - naturally so incognito, just like „Herr Wolf" had come to the Obersalzberg for the first time.

*The smoking remnants of the Berghof after the bombing raid of 25 April 1945. Six years earlier, after his success against Austria, Czechoslovakia and Poland, Hitler bragged and threatened: „We have always played Vabanque ('Bet the Bank'), and will always play Vabanque. For the good of the German people, we must strive towards war every 15 to 20 years."*

Photo: Archive Dr. Feulner

*In May 1930, the postal service inaugurated a bus line along the modestly built road from Berchtesgaden up to the Obersalzberg. Against this development arose resistance: Such auto traffic disturbs a fabulous holiday area with noise, exhaust and dust. In the photo a postal bus from 1930 midway up the Obersalzberg. The dramatic course of history after 1933 allowed only the high alpine backdrop to remain.*

Photo: Archive Dr. Feulner

*Hitler left nothing to coincedence concerning an effective self-portrayal. In countless photographic series he posed - according to need - as self confident Führer (as here), as demagogic speaker, or as imperturbable head of state. Hitler's most rigorous self-portrayal was undoubtedly the Word, as the quotes on the following page attest.*                                                                                              *Photo: State Archives*

# Adolf Hitler Literally

## Politics, Force and Power

„The art of real demagogues throughout time has therein consisted of always concentrating the attention of the people on a sole adversary. (Thereby) the truth content does not count when facing success." (Mein Kampf)

„The German people need a Peace, not supported through the palm leaves of tearful pacifist mourners, but a service to the World established through the triumphant sword of a higher culture master race." (Mein Kampf)

„One cannot recover lost territory through the verbal proficiency of sharpened parliamentary muzzles, one has to conquer them through a sharpened sword; therefore, through a bloody fight." (Mein Kampf)

„We must be cruel. We must regain the good conscience to cruelty. Only in this way can we expel the geniality and evening cocktail bliss of our people." (25.8.32)

„Whoever stands in our way will be massacred." (28.2.1933)

„The conquest of power is a process which is never, ever finished. (That requires) continual education and the control of our people." (21.5.35)

„Only means of force provide a solution to the German question; this can never be without risk. It is my irrevocable decision to quickly subjugate Austria and Czechoslovakia. Therewith the Reich gains the nutritional base for an additional 12 million people, which presupposes the compulsory emigration of two million people from Czechoslovakia and one million from Austria." (5.11.37)

„The solution of political problems is not possible without intrusion into foreign states or attacking foreign property." (23.5.39)

„It is impossible for us to want to manufacture everything we need through synthetic processes. One must conquer that which one does not have." (20.6.41)

„It was always my habit to have the last word. And all our adversaries can be convinced: The Germany of once laid down their weapons around a quarter to twelve - by principle I always fundamentally stop at five minutes after twelve!" (11.11.42)

## The Führer Principle and Democracy

„I alone lead the movement and nobody places conditions upon me, as long as I personally carry the responsibility. And I bear the total responsibility for everything which occurs in the Movement." (6.3.1925)

„Thus I now proclaim the right to political infallability for myself and my successors in the Party." (4.6.30)

„Here you see an organization built on the thought of absolute authority of the leadership in all areas - the only party which has totally overcome democratic thoughts." (26.2.32)

„Every propaganda has to be popular and must adjust its mental level according to the capacity of the most limited." (30.7.32)

„The precepts of National Socialists: The Führer is always right! ... The program should be dogma; it demands utmost devotion to the Movement! ...Proper is what serves the Movement and therewith Germany! ...The Führer Corps is responsible for the total penetration of the German people in the National Socialist spirit....The Führer's will is the foremost law of the Party." (Official party handbook of 1936.)

„ The democratic Parliament was introduced by the Jew who has conceived this idiocy! „ (30.1.37)

„Every institutuion of this Reich stands under the order of the uppermost political leadership. The Party leads the Reich politically, the armed forces defend it militarily. There is nobody in a responsible position in this state who doubts that I am the authorized leader of the Reich." (Hitler about Hitler, 20. 1. 38)

„It is insanity to imagine today that political views would have to be tolerant. There is no tolerance in nature. Nature is the most intolerant thing that exists." (26. 5. 44)

## War and power

„Each military act in Europe stands - also in the event of its complete success, measured in its sacrifices - in no relation to the possible final gain." (17. 5. 33.)

„I therewith present the following tasks: 1. The German army must be deployable in four years; 2. The German economy must be capable of war in four years." (Secret memorandum of August 1936.)

„Circumstances have forced me for decades to talk almost exclusively about peace. Such peace propaganda can lead only too easily to the interpretation that the present regime wants to maintain peace at all costs." (10. 11. 1938)

„If England wants to have war, then they will have it. It will become a war of destruction like no imagination can envision." (19. 4. 39)

„Wars have always been ended only through destruction of the adversary. Anyone who thinks differently is irresponsible." (23. 11. 39)

„Nobody will ask about the violation of the neutrality of Belgium and Holland if we are victorious." (23. 11. 39)

„The British and French accepted everything in Munich (conference awarding the Sudeten region to Germany): like weaklings they gave-in to my general demands. Under such provisions, it was actually difficult to start a war" (which was supposed to be averted). (21. 2. 45).

## The East and „Living Space"

„We stop the eternal Germanic thrust to the South and West of Europe and direct our vision towards land in the East. If we talk about new land and territory, we can think only about Russia and its subservient border states. But first it is necessary to destroy France." (Mein Kampf)

„One never forgets, however, that the regents of the present Russia are bloodstained common criminals, a scum of mankind, who eradicated millions of their leading intelligentsia in wild bloodgreed; and who exercise the most cruel, tyrannical rule of all times. These rulers belong to a people who in a rare mixture enjoin bestial cruelty with the incomprehensible art of lies." (Mein Kampf)

„The war is only able to be conducted if the entire armed forces are nourished in the third year of war (1943) from Russia. Herewith unquestionably 'X' millions of people will starve if what is necessary for us is removed from the country." (2. 5. 41)

„We will therefore emphasize again, that we were forced (after the attack on the USSR) to occupy an area, to regulate, and to secure it. Nevertheless, we'll take all necessary measures: shootings, evacuating, etc. Fundamentally, it depends on handily dissecting the gigantic cake (= USSR), whereby we can initially master, secondly manage and thirdly exploit them. The partisan war also has its advantages: it gives us the possibility to eradicate whatever places itself against us." (16. 7. 41)

„The fight over world hegemony will be decided for Europe through the possession of Russian territory; it makes Europe the most blockade-secure area in the World." (18. 9. 41)

„Stalin is one of the greatest living persons because he made it possible, through the hardest measures, to forge a state out of this Slavic rabbit family." (23. 9. 41)

„There is (in the East) only one task: a Germanization through German take-over, and to consider the natives as red Indians. We completely eliminate the destructive Jew." (17. 10. 41)

„Russia is unquestionably the richest country on the earth. Besides, the most important raw material is at Russia's disposal: people. The Ukraine is Europe's India" (meant as British colony). (10. 12. 41)

„Nobody brings us out of the East anymore! We had a potash monopoly. We now gain a bread,coal, irons, and wood monopoly." (4. 2.42)

## Forced Laborers

„In the occupied areas we master at the moment, and which contain more than 250 million people, we will also make every last man work for us." (9.11.41)

On Hitler's order, a new form of job creation was arranged on 18.9.42: „Extradition of anti-social elements from the penal system to the Reichs SS Commander for extermination through work. Those in custodial security (Author's Note: concentration camp prisoners) will be delivered, among them: Jews, gipsys, Russians, Ukrainians, Poles with more than 3 years punishment, Czechs or Germans with over 8 years punishment."

„Whether the other people live in prosperity or whether they perish due to starvation - that interests me only in so far as we need them as slaves for our culture. Whether during construction of tank trenches 10,000 Russian women collapse from exhaustion only interests me in so far as the tank trench for Germany will be finished." (Himmler at Posen on 4.10.43 in reference to the Führer's will.)

## Political Actions in Europe

„I am the last chance for Europe! The new Europe will not be exacted through parliamentary ballots, also not through discussions and resolutions, but solely through Force." (26. 2. 45)

„If the Italians would have kept their paws out of this war! Italy's entry into the war led almost automatically to the first victories of our adversaries! We have everything to lose, but nothing to win, if we bind ourselves to weaklings who have already demonstrated their inconsistencies during earlier tests. With the Romanic people, weakness effectively mates with absurd pretentiousness." (17. 2. 45)

„The rearmament is as good as finished. Thus am I determined — beginning with a lightning-like, quick attack on Austria and Czechoslovakia — to secure a larger living space for the Germans in Europe through Force." (5. 11. 37)

„It is my irrevocable decision to smash Czechoslovakia in the foreseeable future through a militarily action." (Hitler's decree of 30. 5. 38)

Hitler on 26. 9. 38, relating to negotiations with Chamberlain over the annexation of the Sudeten area: „I have assured him that the German people want nothing other than peace. I have further assured him, and repeat it here, that if this problem is solved, there is no longer a territorial problem for Germany in Europe; (and that) I am then no longer interested in the Czech state! And that will be guaranteed to him! We want absolutely no Czechs!"

„The intent of an attack by Germany on Poland is only a lie invented by the international press." (28. 4. 39)

On 22. 8. 39, before army commanders (relating to the impending attack on Poland): „I will provide the propagandist occasion for the declaration of war, regardless whether it is plausible or not. War does not depend on Righteousness, but on Victory. Lock your heart against sympathy, brutality, great hardship! The Stronger has the right." („Operation Tannenberg" offered the occasion whereby the SS - with murdered concentration camp prisoners - instigated a „Polish attack" on radio transmitters at Gleiwitz.)

„Germany has solemnly insured Belgium and Holland that it is ready to acknowledge these states any time as inviolable neutral areas and to guarantee this." (30. 1. 37).

„The Dutch and Belgian air bases must be occupied militarily. No declaration of neutrality can be granted." (23. 5. 39)

Holland, Belgium and Luxemburg were invaded on 10. 5. 40, under the pretext of acting against the attack plans of France and England „to ensure the neutrality of the aforementioned countries by force of arms".

## *Treaties and International Law*

„An alliance whose goal does not include the intention of war is meaningless and worthless". (Mein Kampf)

„Two things enable one to unite people: common ideals and common treachery."
(1. 8. 23)

„ I would like to testify in the name of the national government and the entire national assembly, that we too share the deepest understanding for the same feelings and founded claim to lifestyle as other people. I do not intend to Germanize those who are not Germans; and thereby I respect the rights of other people." (17. 5. 33)

„The German Reichs government will painfully observe each voluntarily signed treaty." (21. 5. 35) Nevertheless, from 1933 onward, Hitler's Germany had broken 84 international treaties.

„One should strive to achieve a crushing or decisive blow against the adversary at the war's beginning. Hereby considerations assume no role over righteousness and injustice or treaties." (23. 5. 39)

„Treaties are only to be observed as long as they fulfill a purpose." (16. 7. 40)

## *Racism and Jews*

„The Jew is the likeness of the devil. Judaism means the racial tuberculosis of the people." (March 1923)

„What we see before us today as human culture is the exclusively creative product of the Aryans, (who) absolutely were the sole founders of a higher race, and consequently the original version of that which we understand by the word `Human´." (Mein Kampf)

„The Jew forms the most powerful contrast to the Aryan. He is the parasite in the body of other people. The dominion of the inferior, however, is the Jew." (Mein Kampf)

„During the war 1914-1918, if one would have held even 12 or 15 thousand of these Hebrew folk-ruiners under poison gas, like hundreds of thousands our very best workers in the field, then the millions of victims at the Front would have not been futile: 12 thousand scoundrels eliminated at the proper time would have spared the lives of perhaps a million valuable Germans." (Mein Kampf)

„The span which lies between the lowest, yet still so-called 'people' and our supreme Race is greater than that between the most primitive human and the supreme monkey." (Reichs Party Convention 1933)

„The discovery of the Jewish virus is one the greatest revolutions. We will recover our health only if we eradicate the Jew. I feel like a Robert

Koch of politics. I have exposed the Jews as a germ which undermines society." (16. 4. 41)

„The soldier in the East is not only a fighter according to the rules of war, but also the porter of an inexorable national idea and an avenger for all bestialities which were afflicted upon the German nationality. Therefore the soldier must have a full understanding for the necessity of the hard, but just atonement against the Jewish sub-race." (Order of the Day by Field Marshal General von Reichenau on 10. 10. 1941. Hitler found this order to be „excellent", and expanded it to the entire Army of the East).

Hitler also praised the Order of the Day by Field Marshal General von Manstein on 20.11.1941: „Judaism further forms the cell for all disturbances and possible uprisings. The Jewish- Bolshevist system must be forever eradicated."

From the record of a conference with Hitler in August 1942 concerning the „Final Solution of the Jewish question". Thereby the accountant of the „final solution" in Poland, SS Commander and former Viennese Gauleiter Odilo Globocnik, expounded (referring to mass burial of the abundantly murdered Jews): „Gentlemen, if another generation should come after us which is so weak and so cowardly that they do not understand our great task (Author's Note: annihilation of the Jews), then all of National Socialism has been for nothing. I am on the contrary of the opinion that one should set bronze plaques, with the inscription that we have had the courage to complete this great and necessary achievement." Hitler's commentary: „Good Globocnik, that is indeed also my view!".

„This struggle (Author's Note: World War II) will therefore not end with the destruction of Aryan mankind, but with the extermination of Jewry in Europe. We will only attain health if we eradicate the Jew." (24. 2. 43)

„National Socialism expelled the Jews to cleanse the German living space of the Jewish poison. This was a necessary, life-saving detoxification cure. I have not left the Jews - with their projecting noses and vice-ridden nostrils - in the uncertainty that this vermin is finally eradicated in Europe." (3. 2. 45)

„In a morally - more and more through the Jewish poison - contaminated world, one will be eternally grateful to National Socialism that I have eradicated the Jews in Central Europe." (2. 4. 45)